CONTENTS

ACKNOWLEDGMENTS vii

PART ONE 1

*When the Rules Don't Work, Change the Game:
Why Direct Calling Works When Nothing Else Does*

CHAPTER ONE 3

This Used to Be Easy—What Happened?
Learn why it's often tough to get a job, why it isn't your fault, and why
today's job market is so challenging and unpredictable.

CHAPTER TWO 15

When the Old Rules Don't Work—Break Them
In today's market, when most of the jobs are "invisible," the
direct-calling strategy is the proven way to get a great job.

CHAPTER THREE 29

Should You Still Use Traditional Job-Hunting Techniques?
Find out how to supplement your search by using networking, job boards, and
other "old-fashioned" techniques in a smart and time-efficient way.

PART TWO 47

The Fifteen-Day Direct-Calling Campaign:
Your Game Plan for Success

CHAPTER FOUR 49

Identify Your Targets—And Know What They Want
Well before you pick up the phone, your successful direct-calling
campaign begins with a well-organized research program.

CHAPTER FIVE 67

Making Contact: Your Fifteen-Day Action Plan
Your mission: fifteen days of intense effort. Your goal: three
interviews in three weeks. Your reward: a job.

PART THREE 93

Following Through: How to Nail the Job

CHAPTER SIX 95

The Phone Interview
Discover how to turn an initial phone conversation into the
face-to-face meeting that could land you a job.

CHAPTER SEVEN 115

The Face-to-Face Interview
Be prepared to make the best possible impression in your interview, and learn
how to counter even the toughest of questions with a winning response.

GET HIRED FAST!

Tap the Hidden Job Market
in 15 Days

Brian Graham

Adams Media
Avon, Massachusetts

For Brenda

Published by Adams Media, an F+W Publications Company
57 Littlefield Street, Avon, MA 02322
www.adamsmedia.com

ISBN: 1-59337-263-9
Printed in Canada.

J I H G F E D C B

Library of Congress Cataloging-in-Publication Data
Graham, Brian.
Get hired fast! / Brian Graham.
    p.   cm.
ISBN 1-59337-263-9
1. Job hunting. 2. Employment interviewing. I. Title.
HF5382.7.G697 2005
650.14—dc22

2004025973

This publication is designed to provide accurate and authoritative information with
regard to the subject matter covered. It is sold with the understanding that the pub-
lisher is not engaged in rendering legal, accounting, or other professional advice. If legal
advice or other expert assistance is required, the services of a competent professional
person should be sought.

—From a *Declaration of Principles* jointly adopted by a Committee of the
American Bar Association and a Committee of Publishers and Associations

Many of the designations used by manufacturers and sellers to distinguish their products are claimed as trademarks. Where those designations appear in this book and
Adams Media was aware of a trademark claim, the designations have been printed with
initial capital letters.

This book is available at quantity discounts for bulk purchases.
For information, please call 1-800-872-5627.

CHAPTER **EIGHT** 133

What If They Say Yes? What If They Say No?

You can turn that hoped-for job offer into an even better job, and you can even convert a job rejection into a positive for your career.

PART **FOUR** 151

Take Control of Your Future: How to Enhance Your Job Security—And Your Long-Term Career Security

CHAPTER **NINE** 153

Keeping Your New Job Once You Get It

Make yourself indispensable from the first day you start your new job.

CHAPTER **TEN** 165

The New Reality: Keep Looking, Even When You Have a Job

With the days of a one-company career long gone, you need to learn how to continually develop new and better job opportunities.

INDEX 181

ACKNOWLEDGMENTS

This project began at the suggestion of Doug Wolf, author or co-author of more than thirty outstanding books. Thank you, Doug, for the insight and recommendations that became the foundation for this work.

Thanks are also due to my agent, Margot Maley Hutchison of Waterside Productions, for her support and trust in a first-time author. I am also grateful to my editor, Jill Alexander of Adams Media, for immediately recognizing the potential of this new and exciting job-hunting approach, and for enthusiastically embracing this project. Many thanks to her and the team at Adams Media for making this book a reality. Thanks also to Alison Blake for her knowledge, intuition, and guidance in preparing this manuscript.

I want to express my appreciation to eleven leaders in the human resources and recruiting professions who shaped and influenced my thinking, and subsequently the content of this book: Dick Domanski, VP of Human Resources at ADP; Mark Smith and Alma Tcruz, human resources consultants; Andrea Jupina, successful author and founder of Andrea Jupina Associates; Chris Reardon, Senior Director of Staffing at Exel Logistics; Jim Armstrong, former Director of Human Resources at Sequent Computer Systems; Twilla Skelton, VP of Staffing at ACS, Inc.; Jim Lang, founder, Jim Lang and Associates; Jeff Simmons, Director of Executive Search, Wal-Mart Stores, Inc.; Pam Ferrell, Manager of Bringing in Really "Cool" Talent, Texas Instruments, Inc. (her actual title!); and Bill Donovan, Founder and

CEO of Proviture, Inc. I am indebted to all of you for the opportunities you gave me, and the experiences we shared. The knowledge I gained as a result of our association contributed greatly to the content of this work.

An undertaking like this is not possible without the support of family and friends. I'd like to thank my parents, John and Sally Graham, and my mother-in-law, Zita Wiebler, for their unwavering confidence and their support of this project. Thanks also to my eight brothers, who have contributed indirectly to this work: Scott, John Jr., Andy, Bruce, Doug, Don, Dave, and Mike. (My next book should be about you guys—oh, the stories I could tell!) I'd also like to thank my good friend Brent Roberts for his contribution to this book. To my daughters Claire and Lucy—without even trying, you make life special, and I am so proud of both of you. And most of all, special thanks to my beautiful wife Brenda for her encouragement, insight, sense of humor, and support during this project. You're lucky if once in a lifetime you meet someone special enough to change your life for the better. I was fortunate enough to marry that person, and my deepest thanks go to her.

PART ONE

When the Rules Don't Work,

Change the Game: *Why Direct Calling*

Works When Nothing Else Does

CHAPTER ONE

This Used to Be Easy—What Happened?

Last time you needed a job, you posted your resume on Monster.com and got six calls the first day. You're just as qualified now—but the phone isn't ringing. This chapter will explain why jobs can be hard to find, and why you need to adapt your job-search strategies to uncover the ones that are out there.

Remember the "good old days"? A few years ago, finding a job was simple: You posted your resume on Monster.com, put the word out to your friends, sent hard copies of your resume to a few companies, and got in touch with the recruiters who'd been pestering you for months. Then you ordered a pizza, sat down with a good book, and waited for the phone to ring.

Usually, you didn't have to wait long. Back then, employers hired nearly everyone in sight, and workers—especially those in high-tech jobs—could name their price. With the dot-com boom in full swing, and employment hovering at 4 percent (and only 1.3 percent in places like Silicon Valley), employers were desperate, offering huge signing bonuses and high salaries to anyone with skills. They'd even pay their staff thousands of dollars just for referring new employees.

That was then. Now, just a few years later, it's a new world. Fortunately, we're emerging from the shadow of the latest recession and recovering from the terrible hits our country took at the start of the new millennium: the tragedy of September 11, the dot-com crash, the scandals that brought down major corporations. Hiring is picking up, and we're getting back to normal—but it's a "new normal," and the job market will never be the same again.

Hope on the Horizon?

All signs indicate that the job market will be unpredictable for several years to come. Even experts can't forecast what's going to happen over the short term, because so many forces are acting on the economy and the employment market. However, one thing seems fairly certain: If you can hang on until 2010 or so, you'll probably have it made. That's because Baby Boomers are hitting retirement age, and, before the decade is out, they'll leave millions of job slots empty. The National Association of Manufacturers recently released a white paper forecasting a "skilled worker gap" that will begin appearing in 2005 and increase to 5.3 million workers by 2010, and 14 million by 2020. Generations X and Y are simply too small to replace that many employees. Thus, with luck, the job seekers of the year 2010 will get to turn the tables on employers, and once again call the tune when it comes to salaries, perks, and benefits.

Why? For one reason, we're learning how to be more productive—that is, how to do the same amount of work (or even more) with fewer resources, including fewer people. Hundre ds of new technologies, from self-serve grocery lines to self-restoring computer networks, are allowing companies to cut staffs without cutting service. That's good news for corporations, but it's bad news for highly qualified people who suddenly find themselves out of a job.

Another seismic shift is occurring as a result of globalization, with millions of other people finding that their jobs are still needed—but not in the United States. America is now in the throes of a "structural" change in the job market, with hundreds of thousands of information technology, software engineering, manufacturing, and call center jobs leaving America for India, China, and other offshore sites. Gartner, a top research firm, predicts that in the very near future, one out of every ten jobs with U.S.–based information-technology vendors or service providers will move out of the country; Forrester Research predicts that, by the year 2015, an additional 3.3 million white-collar jobs will move overseas. And the losses are not confined to the tech sector. Manufacturing and call center jobs are being outsourced, while other fields such as accounting, architecture, medical dictation, and even radiology are losing jobs to offshoring.

That leaves more people, many of them highly qualified and accustomed to excellent salaries and great benefits, scrambling for the dwindling number of jobs that can't be outsourced. The result is that many people with expensive college degrees and years of experience are finding it nearly impossible to get a job. Of course, if you're one of these people, you don't need to be told this. You're living it firsthand.

Is It Going to Get Better?

Yes and no. In general, it looks like the bear market for job hunters is over. But many of the jobs lost due to structural changes aren't coming back in quantity any time soon.

While some fields will prosper for the foreseeable future—now is a great time to be a nurse or a home health care provider, for instance—people in many formerly "bulletproof" fields, from accounting to architecture to financial advising, are discovering that the economic rebound isn't translating into easy job-hunting. And many people who are currently employed are finding that even in a job market recovery, their companies still expect long hours of overtime work in exchange for inadequate wages and benefits—a fact that's likely to be true for some time to come.

Even though the large-scale Baby-Boomer retirement will ease job market strains down the road, that's little consolation for people who need a job now. If you're in a field hard-hit by restructuring, automation, or outsourcing, it could be a buyer's market for the next few years when it comes to hiring.

Where Does That Leave You?

If you're one of the millions of Americans looking for a job, or you're trapped in a dead-end job you hate, the current situation leaves you in trouble if you're relying solely on traditional job-hunting techniques. The tried-and-true methods that always worked before aren't working as well any more for people in job fields undergoing structural changes, and they aren't likely to work in the future—at least the near future. That's because as the job market changes, so do the hiring methods of companies and the strategies of recruiters.

Here are four recent changes in the hiring process that have made traditional job-search techniques ineffective for many people:

Change #1: Human resources departments often won't read your resume

Four years ago, if you sent a resume to the human resources department of a company, you had a good chance of getting a call, especially if you worked in a high-tech field. Today, however, you may be going up against hundreds, or even thousands, of highly qualified candidates who are doing the same thing. Even a strong resume may not help you, because many HR departments were pared to the bone during the recent recession, leaving almost no one to manage the daily flood of letters and e-mails from job seekers. In bad economic times, administrative workers who don't directly generate revenue often get cut in the first round of layoffs. Frequently, HR staffs are severely downsized, and some smaller companies eliminate their HR staffs almost entirely—a trend that takes time to reverse, even when the economy picks up.

This has two consequences. One, of course, is that fewer people are available to screen resumes and identify good prospects. Another more subtle effect is that, with fewer in-house recruiters (or, often, none at all) focusing on long-term corporate goals, companies lose their vision and hire only enough people to keep the day-to-day operations going. Other goals—bringing in new talent with a fresh perspective or keeping a company on the cutting edge of its industry—go out the window. It's shortsighted, and eventually it will hurt these businesses, but for now it's a fact of life.

However, corporate shortsightedness isn't the only reason that your resume won't land on the desk of the person you need to impress. Another reason is that in the age of the Internet, it's easy for job seekers to shotgun resumes to hundreds of companies. The result is an avalanche of applications for every open position, and even corporations with healthy human resources staffs can't begin to give serious consideration to the stacks of resumes they receive. Intel, for example, gets 15,000 to 20,000 resumes each month, and Google receives 1,000 every day.

Most large companies feed these resumes into automated Applicant Tracking Systems that parse the information and feed it into a database. If you've used the right formatting tricks, which are discussed later on in the book, the facts on your resume will probably make it in there—but so will data from thousands of other candidates. Hidden in amongst that mass of bits and bytes, your resume will be as lost as the proverbial needle in a haystack.

Worse yet, the data in Applicant Tracking Systems quickly becomes unwieldy, so HR staffs often purge "old" resumes after a few months. The result is that thousands of resumes never make it into a database, or are deleted before ever being read by a human being. Thus, of the hundreds of carefully crafted letters and resumes you're likely to send during your quest for a job, only one or two dozen—if you're lucky— are going to get a serious reading.

Using a company's online application process is equally frustrating. Most online forms force you to strip your accomplishments down to bare bones ("check your three primary skill areas," "list your last two positions") so that your data can be parsed electronically, meaning that you'll sound no different or better than every other sales manager or Web designer who's applying for a job.

Change #2: Recruiters might not be much help

Don't count on third-party recruiters to find you a job. Today's recruiters are inundated with resumes, and it's their job to field a few candidates quickly—not to wade through all those resumes to find the *best* candidates. You'll probably find to your dismay that the same recruiters who cultivated you during the boom times won't give you the time of day now, if you're in a field that's no longer in huge demand.

——— TALE from the TRENCHES ———

I spoke recently with a senior level accountant who had interviewed with three prospective employers. "Most of the interviewers acted as if they were doing me a favor by even talking with me," he told me. "Things sure have changed since a few years ago." He told me that two of the companies never provided any follow-up at all after his interviews. The final company sent him a "thanks, but no thanks" e-mail.

His story is one of thousands with the same theme. Only a select number of companies, and a select number of recruiters, do the right thing by treating applicants as politely during candidate gluts as they do during candidate shortages.

This might seem unfair, but look at it from the recruiter's point of view. If a recruiter gets 120 resumes from technical writers, and the first dozen resumes in that stack are excellent, the payoff for wading through the rest of the stack is almost nonexistent. A few years ago, the jobs-to-candidates ratio was so high that recruiters could place virtually any qualified employee in a good position, so they took nearly all comers and worked at cultivating long-term relationships with many of their candidates. Now, with the pool of jobs dwindling in several once-hot fields, recruiters are scrambling to attract employers rather than candidates, because the latter (unfortunately for job hunters) are in good supply.

Change #3: Job boards aren't what they used to be

A few years ago, you could get a job within weeks (or even days) simply by posting your resume on Monster, Dice, FlipDog, or other job boards. It wasn't unusual for candidates in high-demand fields to get a dozen calls on the first day of posting a resume.

These days, however, you may be shocked when you visit the job boards, list your keywords, and hit the "search" button. If you're in one of the fields undergoing cataclysmic shifts due to mechanization or outsourcing, you'll probably discover that instead of hundreds of listings in your field, there are only a few dozen that appear to fit your skills—if you're lucky. You're also likely to discover that a significant percentage of these listings are for jobs that are already filled.

There are a number of reasons for this. One reason, of course, is that in a number of fields affected by structural changes, there are fewer job openings overall. Another is that with human resources departments decimated in recent years, most HR staffs are so overworked that maintaining job boards is now a low-level priority. Many positions never get posted at all, many others do not accurately reflect the jobs they're advertising, and many never get removed when they're filled.

As a result, the number of real positions advertised on job boards can be depressingly small (and often does not accurately reflect the actual number of openings at the firms posting the jobs). Frequently, highly qualified job hunters respond to dozens or even hundreds of listings without ever getting a call. And the best jobs often go unnoticed, because many postings are so poorly written (how often have you looked at a job posting and thought, "What *are* they asking for?") that job-seekers skip right over them.

Change #4: Networking isn't always effective anymore

Many experts tell you that networking with friends, relatives, former colleagues, college roommates, neighbors, and acquaintances is the most effective tool for locating a new job. That used to be true, but for many people it isn't now.

Why? Because if you're in a field that's been hit by restructuring, many of your friends and colleagues are in the same boat that you are, and they're more concerned about their own careers than yours. Moreover, as you'll see in the next chapter, the vast majority of jobs are "hidden" jobs—jobs that are never advertised in the paper, never posted on job boards, and never even mentioned internally at companies—so even your most well-intentioned friends won't be able to steer you to them.

Try All the Traditional Techniques—But Don't Count on Them

The bottom line is that when you use traditional job-hunting measures in today's job market, there's a good chance you'll come up empty-handed—especially if you're seeking not just a job, but a great job. Not that you shouldn't use these techniques. You should. In fact, you should use them vigorously (more on this in Chapter Three). Post your resume on every major job board, and check to see if there are specialty boards for your career field or your city. Talk to your friends, your relatives, your former coworkers, people at the gym, your next-door neighbor, even your doctor or your hairdresser. But don't expect it to work, because the traditional hiring process is broken.

---------------- **T**ALE from the **TRENCHES** ----------------

One experienced software developer lost his job at the end of 2000 when his company cancelled his project. He posted three resumes online, and sent out a few e-mails to local firms. Within three hours, he got six calls. By the end of the week, he had two outstanding offers on the table and several more in the offing. When the same software developer wound up job-hunting again in late 2001, he posted his resume on more than a dozen job boards, contacted every technical recruiter in his city, and e-mailed more than fifty companies. In four months, he got ten calls, three interviews, and only one job offer—at $20,000 less than his previous salary. He took the job, because he was desperate and needed the money. Today, with the market picking up, he's getting more job offers—but the callers still want long hours, and the salaries they're offering will barely cover his bills.

In reality, the hiring process has always been "broken" in many ways, but the boom market for job hunters covered up many of the defects. Those in staffing and human resources talked for years about fixing the system, but ultimately they didn't do anything because, with so much demand for all levels of talent, nobody got hurt by an inefficient process.

Now, however, you're the one who's being hurt, if you're in a field where great jobs are hard to get. Even if you dedicate ten hours a day to a traditional job search, it's likely that companies won't respond to you, recruiters won't return your calls, your posts on job boards will fall into a black hole, and your efforts to find a job by traditional means will seem hopeless. And you'll be left wondering: "What do I do now?"

Don't Panic—There IS a Solution!

All of this is very discouraging. It's even more discouraging if you've already spent weeks or months looking for a job, without any luck or even a glimmer of hope on the horizon. And it's equally frustrating if you're working at a job you loathe, with poor benefits, little chance for advancement, and seemingly no chance of finding anything better. If you fall into this latter category, you're not alone. According to a survey conducted in 2003 by the Conference Board, a management think tank, less than half of Americans currently like their jobs—the greatest level of discontent since the group began conducting its survey in 1995. Only one worker in three is happy with his or her wages, and only one in five is happy with the benefits being offered.

But believe it or not, there *is* good news. You're not doomed to be unemployed forever, and you don't need to accept a mediocre job that's not worthy of your talents. There *is* a way to get a great job, if you're willing to try something new. It takes guts and hard work. It isn't for the faint of heart, or people who aren't willing to give 110 percent. But it will dramatically improve your odds of getting the perfect job, if you're willing to commit three weeks of your life to it.

It's direct calling—a method of cutting out the middlemen, and reaching the people who have the "invisible" jobs. In the next three chapters, we'll look at what it is, how it works, and how to implement a Fifteen-Day Direct-Calling Plan that's virtually guaranteed to win you one or more job interviews.

CHAPTER TWO

When the Old Rules Don't Work—Break Them

You know the drill: Send out resumes, scour the job boards, and network with friends and colleagues. All of these strategies may have worked in the past, but they won't work as well now if you're in a field that's short on jobs and swarming with desperate, highly qualified job seekers. You'll still want to use these "old-fashioned" job-hunting techniques, because sometimes they DO work—but to really compete, you need to find the hidden jobs that make up nearly 90 percent of the job market and pursue them aggressively.

As a job hunter, you're conditioned to follow the rules. The most sacred of these rules, followed by generations of job seekers, is: *Never directly call the people with the jobs.* Nowadays, just three little words hold the key to getting the job you want: BREAK THAT RULE!

Why? Because, as Chapter One explains, the indirect approach to job-hunting isn't always effective any more. It worked back when good jobs were stable and plentiful in every field, and before the Internet allowed job hunters to deluge companies with thousands of resumes. In today's world, however, it can be an ineffective strategy if you're in a line of work where good jobs are scarce due to outsourcing, automation, or other changes. Hunting for a job the old-fashioned way, by e-mailing resumes, posting your resume on job boards, or calling recruiters, is like buying a handful of lottery tickets every week. You might be the one person in a hundred who hits pay dirt, but the odds are against you.

The Internet Frenzy

Thanks to the ease of submitting resumes online, more than 92 percent of recruiters and hiring managers polled in a recent survey say that they are deluged with irrelevant responses to job postings. Seventy-one percent say most of the resumes they receive fail to match their job descriptions, making it nearly impossible to find great candidates who get lost in the flood of paper. A chief cause of this problem is "resume spamming." According to John Sumser of the newsletter *Electronic Recruiting News*, under the right circumstances a job hunter can submit around 600 resumes in a ten-hour day of job searching. Moreover, the research indicates that this pace can be sustained, unabated, for about fifteen days (or 9,000 resume submittals). Multiply that by millions of job hunters, and you'll understand why e-mailing companies is almost always an exercise in futility.

Job hunters tend to think that it's their fault when traditional job-search methods don't work for them. In reality, however, their lack of results has nothing to do with their skills or qualifications, and everything to do with a system that doesn't work any more.

The Solution—If You Have the Guts

The good news is that there *is* a way to get a great job. It isn't easy, and it isn't fun. It will be embarrassing and sometimes humiliating. It will test your courage and your persistence. But statistics say it will work.

The solution is to job-hunt using the method that recruiting professionals use. When recruiters want to secure new business with corporate clients, they directly call the companies they're targeting. You can employ the same concept by directly calling hiring managers and other key hiring contacts.

Why subject yourself to an approach that's challenging and stressful, when you could just post resumes and wait for a call? Because, unlike traditional methods of job-hunting, direct calling works astonishingly well. It works better, in fact, than any other job-hunting technique. And that's not just opinion, but a fact based on scientific research.

Says career coach Marky Stein, "Study after study, and my own ten-plus years of experience, have proven that, hands down, cold calling employers is superior to all other methods." Stein cites a study by JIST Works in Philadelphia, which trained 1,000 job hunters to do intensive direct calling during the recession of 1990. Of that group, 66 percent obtained jobs within two and a half weeks, and 90 percent had jobs within ninety days.

Direct calling is the technique that recruiters build their entire careers around, and it's growing in popularity among savvy job seekers as well. A 2002 survey by a New York career-counseling group found that direct calls result in a far greater number of interviews per job-hunting hour than networking does, and polls of successful job seekers consistently show that on average 35 percent got their jobs by directly contacting the company or the hiring manager.

Those numbers aren't surprising, because good managers like to have control over the candidates they interview. They know that the best way to gain that control is to select candidates themselves.

────────── **TALE** from the **TRENCHES** ──────────

When I worked as a hiring manager, I never asked Human Resources to find candidates for me. I found them myself, because I knew the kind of people I wanted, the skills I needed, and the "chemistry" of the teams I managed. In addition, I knew that at the end of the day, I—not the HR staff—would be held accountable for my success or failure. It made far more sense for me to find promising candidates on my own than to have an HR staff, with only secondhand knowledge of my project, try to guess at the type of employee I needed. And I wasn't the only manager who felt that way; a high percentage of the managers with whom I've worked prefer to take recruiting decisions into their own hands.

Early on, we're all taught that the right way to get a foot in the door of a company is to go through the HR department. However, there's no rulebook that says that candidates must be sourced by the HR staff. Many of the best candidates are people who show the initiative and drive to contact a manager directly. Human resources can facilitate the hiring of employees *after* a manager sources them, but thousands of managers, at both large and small companies, find candidates themselves.

It's these managers who hold the key to the huge majority of jobs that aren't publicly advertised. These men and women are busy people who want to hire quickly and efficiently when the need arises, and nearly every one of them keeps a file of potential candidates—not the stack of resumes that's piling up in the HR department, but their own file of personal contacts, including candidates who call them directly. Eighty percent of the time, they'll hire someone whose name is in that file. It's your job to get your name on that list, by transforming yourself from a stranger to a desirable candidate. And the quickest way to do that is by direct calling.

Networking vs. Direct Calling

Networking is the process of contacting people you already know: friends, former colleagues, neighbors, and anyone else who might have a job lead. Of all the traditional job-hunting techniques, networking is the most effective. However, networking doesn't work like it used to. That's particularly true if you're in an industry that's undergoing rapid change and restructuring. You'll probably find that many of your previous firms are out of business, that you no longer have contact numbers for many former colleagues, and that the colleagues you can track down are looking for new jobs themselves. Direct calling, in contrast, means calling people you've never met. The people you'll be contacting are strangers, but they are known quantities in two important ways: they work at companies you're interested in, and they are the key players in the hiring process. Thus, they're infinitely more valuable, from a job-seeking point of view, than your network of known contacts.

I like to compare the direct-calling approach to the blitz in football. Instead of being knocked out of play by a host of protectors standing between you and your target, you're going to head straight for the quarterback—in this case, the person with the job. It's a difficult play, but the reward is huge.

Why Is Direct Calling So Powerful?

Many job hunters are surprised to learn that they should make direct calling their primary strategy. The "fear factor" stops most of them from doing so, but even the braver ones are highly skeptical that it will work. But it does work—and, what's more, it works for both experienced workers and first-time job seekers. Direct calling not only improves the odds of landing a job quickly, it also improves the odds of landing a *good* job. Direct calling is much more effective than other approaches, and here are nine of the reasons why.

Reason #1: Most jobs aren't advertised

Many times the best jobs are not posted and many other positions aren't advertised on job boards until weeks after a decision is made to hire. If you reach a hiring manager or another key contact in a company before a job is publicly advertised, you won't be competing with hundreds of people for a position. Instead, you'll be one of only a handful of people in the early running—or possibly even the only candidate. That gives you a huge edge over people sending in resumes, especially since up to 50 percent of job openings are filled before they're officially posted.

Reason #2: Hiring decisions are often sudden

Hiring managers frequently sit on job openings for weeks or months, and then make a hire almost instantly. Many times, managers will already have someone in mind when they are finally ready to hire. More often than not, particularly in higher-level jobs, the candidate is found by tapping their own sources. These managers bypass dozens of people who have sent in resumes, or who have gone through recruiters, to make a spontaneous choice—and frequently they choose a candidate who has called them directly.

Reason #3: Direct calling eliminates the middle man

The first and toughest goal in your job search is to make contact with a key player in a company's hiring process. Many job seekers never get this far, because—as we've noted—99 percent of resumes never even get read. Think about the number of resumes you've mailed and the number of calls you've received as a result. If you're like most job seekers, the ratio is demoralizing.

By direct calling, you improve your odds hugely, because you bypass the brutal initial screening process that, in addition to elim inating the chaff (unqualified candidates), eliminates most of the wheat (highly qualified candidates) as well. You won't be passed over by a recruiter, or have your resume tossed aside by a human resources staffer, because you'll reach hiring contacts directly.

Reason #4: Managers will take your call out of sheer curiosity

Some hiring managers have no problem saying, "Not interested!" and hanging up in your ear, but most people are innately curious and it's hard for them to brush off a well-informed, respectful, and courteous caller—even if it's a stranger. Instead, they'll frequently decide to give you a few minutes. In many cases that's all the time you'll need, because the techniques outlined in this book will allow you to make a powerful case for yourself in a very short time.

Direct calling shows that you have initiative. Hiring managers get where they are by being assertive, take-charge people, and they like that attitude in their employees as well. Most of them will admire you, if only secretly, for being brave enough to call them. They'll also be impressed by your ability to assertively pursue a goal. As you talk with them, they're likely to visualize you applying this same fortitude and diligence to a role on their team.

Reason #5: Direct calling can generate referrals

Often it's not your initial call that gets you a job, but a referral from the first company to another firm that's hiring. This is a corollary of the "most people are polite" rule. When a contact wants to get rid of you, but wants to be helpful (or at least doesn't want to seem rude), the individual will frequently say, "Check with So-and-So— I just heard that they have openings." Because these tips are often based on personal conversations between managers, they can steer you to job openings that aren't advertised publicly.

TALE from the TRENCHES

In an article in the *California Job Journal*, writer Rich Heintz describes how he listened to the advice of a career counselor, and focused his recent job-hunting efforts on making direct calls to potential employers. "People were incredibly helpful," he says. "Most offered suggestions. Many provided encouragement—'I was unemployed once. I know what that's like. Good luck!' Truth is, most people want to help." And help they did. Heintz says it took only five calls to get a hit! The contact didn't have any jobs to offer, but referred Heintz to another association with an opening. He called, and got an interview for a $60,000-a-year job with a statewide association.

In effect, by making contact with a single key individual in a single company, you indirectly make contact with his or her network of colleagues as well—and that's a powerful way to tap into the "hidden" job market.

Reason #6: Direct calling allows you to play to your strengths

It's hard to format a resume in a manner that showcases your strong points, especially if your resume is automatically scanned into an Applicant Tracking System that reduces it to a few dry digitized facts. When you call an employer directly, however, *you control the information you present, and the order in which you present it.* This empowers you to emphasize the facts that prove that you deserve consideration.

For instance, if you're currently working in a "stop loss" job that you took because work was scarce and you needed to pay the bills, it's unlikely that this job is a good indication of your talents and experience. A hiring manager who pulls up your resume from an Applicant Tracking System and sees that you're currently working in technical support, for instance, isn't likely to keep reading long enough to find out that you're also an outstanding SQL developer.

Now, imagine the same scenario, but imagine that instead of sending a resume, you call the same hiring manager and say:

> "I noticed in last week's *Info World* that you're expanding into the area of inventory control. I have ten years of experience in developing inventory control systems, and I've been involved in the full development cycle of two major systems for just-in-time inventory control that currently are used by major corporations. In fact, *Info World* gave outstanding reviews to both products . . ."

Clearly, the second approach is vastly more likely to earn you an interview. The hiring manager is sure to note, eventually, that you're currently working in a lower-level position. But in light of your successful track record, that information will appear much less important.

Reason #7: Direct calling is effective if you're changing careers

If your manufacturing job was outsourced to China, or your grocery checking job is now being performed by an automatic scanner, it's possible that you're looking not just for a new job but a new career field. When you're in this situation, it can be difficult to prove on a resume that you're qualified for a new line of work. Even if hiring managers do take a look at your resume (a long shot to begin with), they're likely to skim the section on your recent job experience, and think, "This person isn't qualified, because these jobs all require a different skill set."

If you're in this circumstance, calling a hiring manager directly will allow you to reframe your experience in a way that dramatically plays up your qualifications. To prove the point, let's take the somewhat unusual example of a grocery checker who wants to switch to a career in horticulture. Sounds like a stretch, doesn't it? That's what a hiring manager will think, too, especially if the manager is reading a resume that starts by listing the candidate's last three jobs at Safeway, Wal-Mart, and Costco.

Now, let's see how direct calling works in the same situation. Here's what the candidate's script sounds like:

> "Hello, Ms. Jackson, thank you for taking my call. I read in the *Tribune* that you're opening three new plant nurseries in the metro area, and that you're also planning to offer horticulture classes for

your customers. I've just completed a Master Gardener Course at the agricultural extension, and I've spent six years as a volunteer instructor at the Inner City Green Space Program, so I have a great deal of expertise both in gardening and in teaching children and adults about horticulture. While I'm currently working as a grocery clerk, I'm very interested in (etc.)"

Our candidate effectively makes her current job a nonissue, by demonstrating up front that she has the experience needed for her new choice of career. In fact, there's a good chance that by the time her conversation ends, she'll be a front-runner for the job.

Reason #8: Direct calling makes you memorable

Picture yourself as the hiring manager at an exclusive clothing store, flipping through dozens of resumes from candidates applying for positions as personal shopping assistants. After the first thirty or forty pages, you find yourself struggling to concentrate. Did Candidate Number One have extensive experience in selling to an upscale clientele, or was it Candidate Number Fifteen? What makes Candidate Number Twelve different from Candidate Number Twenty? Who had the degree from Vassar? Which one majored in fashion design?

Now, imagine that the phone rings, you answer it, and a pleasant voice says,

> "Ms. Jones? I noticed in the *Business Journal* that you're interested in expanding your staff of personal shopping assistants, and that you're hoping to attract a younger clientele to your store. As a former dresser for the road show of several Broadway plays, I have a great deal of experience working with exclusive clients who expect to receive the highest level of service. Also, as I've spent the past several

years surrounded by young stars, I have an excellent feel for what the upscale 'twenty-something' and 'thirty-something' age groups are looking for in fashion."

Who do you think the hiring manager will remember an hour later: the dozens of people whose resumes all seemed to run together, or the one caller who sounded perfect for the job?

Reason #9: Direct calling improves your odds

When you mail resumes and get no feedback, you have no clue why. Is it because no one is reading your resume? Or is it because you aren't portraying your skills as well as you should? Is your resume too long, or too short? Are your keywords helping or hurting you? You'll probably never know, and you'll spend far too much time worrying about "why?" "why not?" and "why me?"

In contrast, every direct call you make will be better than the last one. That's because you'll learn through trial and error, and you'll become better at selling your strong points and compensating for your weaknesses. Sales people call this "learning through failure," and it's a process that leads to success.

In short, direct calling works because it gives you access to jobs that aren't publicized or advertised, and often makes you one of the first candidates in line for these jobs. It eliminates roadblocks, in the form of HR staffs that don't read your resume, Applicant Tracking Systems that bury your data along with that of a thousand other job seekers, or recruiters who don't return your calls. It allows you to take control of the image you project to the people who make hiring decisions. And it enables you to constantly refine and improve your presentation, increasing your chances of success each time you call.

The Catch: It's Hard Work

Succeeding at direct calling, however, isn't easy. Many experts tell you to call hiring managers, but they don't tell you how it's done—and doing it wrong can have disappointing results. To succeed at the direct-calling technique, you need to do it in a professional manner.

The following chapters will show you how to handle direct calling with savvy and finesse. You'll learn exactly how the direct calling approach works, and if you use it as outlined, you'll have highly successful results. The following chapters outline a step-by-step Fifteen-Day Action Plan, complete with charts, scripts, and other tools that will enable you to use the direct-calling technique like a professional.

If you follow this plan, you will be committing yourself to an ambitious project: to call 150 job contacts (or as many as possible) in just fifteen days. Statistics show that in a very difficult job market, fifty calls lead to an average of eight successful contacts, which generally lead to one job interview—meaning that during a "down" job cycle, this campaign will typically result in *three interviews in three weeks*. In a good job market, your odds will be dramatically better—typically, in such a market, for each twenty-five calls, you'll score four successful contacts and one job interview.

Success at direct calling, however, takes preparation and hard work. In the following chapters, you'll learn:

- Why 80 percent of your job search is preparation.

- Where and how to identify key contacts in target companies.

- How to use intensive "Internet mining" techniques to uncover crucial data about each of these target companies.

- How to use this information to get the inside track on jobs.

- How to create a database that will allow quick access to the vital information you'll need to impress contacts during your calls.

Then, when you're ready to begin calling, you'll also learn exactly how to script your calls to hiring managers in advance. You'll have complete confidence and say exactly the right things at the right time. You will learn how to revise your scripts to cover any scenario from voice mail to conversations with contacts' staffers to repeat calls. In addition, this guide will show you how to set realistic goals, stay motivated, and follow your plan through to a successful conclusion. In short, you'll have every tool you need to find—and win—the great job you want.

CHAPTER THREE

*Should You Still Use Traditional
Job-Hunting Techniques?*

Direct calling works when other approaches fail—but that doesn't mean you should abandon networking, job boards, and other "old-fashioned" job-hunting techniques. Instead, you need to learn how to use traditional job searching techniques the smart way. However, not all popular job-search techniques are worthwhile—and some will empty your wallet while leaving you no closer to becoming employed.

Direct calling is the smart way to get a job, and it works when other approaches fail. That doesn't mean, however, that you should ignore other job-hunting techniques altogether. Instead, you'll want to augment your direct-calling campaign by investing a small amount of time—about two hours each week—in the traditional methods, including:

- Searching company Web sites for job listings.

- Checking the job ads in trade journals and newspapers.

- Posting resumes on Internet boards, and checking the boards for job postings.

- Networking with people you know.

To return to the analogy employed earlier, using these techniques is like buying lottery tickets: You can't count on them to pay off, but sometimes they do. Only a minority of resumes posted on Monster, HotJobs, or FlipDog will catch the attention of hiring managers, but yours could be in the right place at the right time. Of hundreds of people who apply for a job on a company Web site, only a few will get a shot at an interview, but that happy group could include you. And although networking is often ineffective if you're in a field that's rife with unemployed colleagues, it still works for quite a few job seekers—and maybe you'll be one of them.

The key is to avoid overinvesting in these strategies. If you spend hour after hour posting resumes on increasingly obscure boards, or searching for ever-more distant friends and colleagues, you'll become a victim of the law of diminishing returns: For each hour you invest, you'll work harder and earn less and less reward.

Instead, focus 90 percent of your effort on the direct calling strategy—in which your odds start out strong and get better each day—and limit your other job search efforts to the "bare bones" strategy outlined in this chapter. Used in moderation, traditional methods can occasionally pay off and won't steal valuable time from your direct-calling campaign. Before you start that campaign, here's how to cover the basics of traditional job-hunting, without wasting excess time on these methods.

Start with Your Resume

You'll need a good resume for both your direct-calling campaign and your traditional job-hunting efforts, so now is the time to get yours in shape. Make sure you have two copies of your resume, one in plain text and one in Word. Build your resume in one of these formats, and copy it to a new file to be converted to the other format.

If you're new to writing resumes, or unfamiliar with Microsoft Word, visit your local library and ask for a book on the basics of computerized resume creation. You can also hire a consultant to write your resume for you, or ask for help from a friend or relative who's well versed in Word. Again, be sure to get both Word and plain-text copies loaded onto your computer.

Whether you write your resume yourself or ask someone else to do it, it needs to be scannable—that is, easily read by a scanner that can parse its data and enter information into an applicant tracking system. To maximize the likelihood that a scanner will read your information accurately, follow these rules:

1. Avoid fancy fonts. Instead, pick a widely used font such as Times, Courier, Arial, Helvetica, Tahoma, or Palatino.

2. Avoid graphics, screens, pictures, and anything else that might confuse a text scanner.

3. Stick with ten-, eleven-, or twelve-point type.

4. Use separate lines to list each section of your contact information (name, address, phone, fax, e-mail address).

5. Keep all information in a single column.

6. Left-justify all text, including your name and address at the top of the resume.

7. Don't use bullets. Instead, use asterisks.

8. Don't use headers or footers.

9. Avoid bold type, italics, and underlines. You can emphasize section headings by using capital letters.

10. Separate headings and paragraphs with a blank line, to help the scanner distinguish between sections.

11. If possible, avoid slash marks or vertical lines. The scanner may interpret these as letters.

Also, when you print out copies of your resume, use white paper, and print the copies on a high-quality printer. If you mail copies of your resume, put them in large (9" x 12") manila envelopes so they'll stay flat. Folds can make lines of text very difficult to scan, and can also jam a scanner that has a paper feeder. If your resume is more than one page long, put your name at the top of each page.

What should your resume say about you?

When it comes to the content of your resume, a few key rules are: Keep it simple, keep it short, and keep it specific. If you're highly experienced, it's tempting to list every project you've ever worked on. Don't. Instead, list your last ten to fifteen years of experience only. If you're new to the job market, on the other hand, list your most important academic achievements, because these will substitute for job experience.

How important are keywords?

Keywords are nouns that describe your skills—for instance, ".NET, C#, C/C++, SQL, Java, ASP, HTML, XML, ATL, MFC, COM, GUI, embedded systems, VBA" for a programmer. Some authorities advise you to create a resume that's brimming with keywords, or even list an entire paragraph of keywords at the top or bottom of your resume. However, if a skill is important enough to mention anywhere in your resume, it'll be spotted by anyone who uses a keyword search to find it.

Make a Good Name for Yourself

If you don't have a professional-sounding e-mail address, get one and use it on your resume. Few potential employers are attracted by e-mail addresses including names such as "lovebunny5" or "terminator." Membership in a professional society such as the IMA (Institute of Management Accountants) often entitles you to a free e-mail account. Depending on your field or specialty, you may want to explore this option.

Also, when choosing an e-mail address, try to keep it short and easy to spell. It's a small detail—but if a hiring manager types your address wrong and the e-mail bounces, you may miss a shot at a good job. And last but not least, check your inbox early and often, so you can pursue every lead quickly.

Typically, people looking for job candidates will search for resumes by title, city or state, and a few job skills critical to each position. These are facts that will naturally appear in your resume, so don't go to extra trouble to fill your pages with an alphabet soup of acronyms. However, do make sure you mention each critical skill when outlining your job experience.

Use the Job Boards—Sparingly

Back before the recent recession, when employers were desperate, you could post your resume on a single board and get dozens of calls. Now, even though the job market is once again picking up, the boards are filled with the resumes of thousands of job seekers, and the odds of yours being seen are slim. One disgruntled job seeker describes the process in the following way, "Picture your resume as a snowflake. Picture your snowflake in a blizzard. Picture someone trying to reach out in that blizzard and grab your snowflake. Got the picture?"

How bad are your odds of getting a job on Monster, Career-Builder, or HotJobs? A survey in the year 2000 by Forrester Research found that only 4 percent of job seekers found their last job on the Internet, and CareerXroads, which monitors Internet recruiting activity, reported that the major companies they surveyed found only 1.4 percent of their employees on Monster, 0.39 percent on HotJobs, 0.29 percent on CareerBuilder, and 0.27 percent on HeadHunter. net. Another sobering statistic for Internet job hunters: On Monster, the ratio of resumes to job posts is currently running about seventeen to one.

Inundated with responses to job board posts, most employers look at only a handful of incoming resumes. To make matters worse, a few job board posts aren't legitimate posts at all, but "pseudo-jobs." Sometimes you'll find that a job board listing for a seemingly perfect job is actually a come-on for a resume spamming service, or even a ploy to involve you in a pyramid sales scheme. Companies will also place ads for positions they have no intention of filling in the near future just to see what kind of candidate pool it will yield.

Even the legitimate job ads that make up the bulk of posts on the job boards are often slapped together by recruiters who receive little or no guidance from HR departments that were gutted by layoffs in recent years. In earlier times, recruiters worked closely with HR personnel to make sure each job posting was a gem that spelled out exactly what a firm wanted. Now more often than not recruiters only get a boilerplate description, which may or may not be an accurate reflection of what the job entails.

So why spend any time working the job boards? Because, if you do it right, it's a strategy that requires almost no effort. Again, the lottery ticket analogy is apt. You're not likely to win the million-dollar prize, but if you only buy a single ticket, you won't lose enough to hurt. Of the hundreds of thousands of job hunters out there right now, at least a few hundred will get jobs almost effortlessly by posting their resumes on job boards, so it's worth gambling a few minutes of your time on this approach.

There are job hunters, however, who invest almost all of their time and energy in finding job boards, posting resumes on these boards, and religiously scouring them, every day, for new leads. They're wasting valuable time, and—like the lottery player who spends hundreds of dollars a week on tickets and is still overwhelmingly likely to lose—they're not substantially improving their odds. To maximize your effort-to-payoff ratio, forget about being a "job board potato" glued to a computer screen 24/7 waiting for a new job lead to appear. Instead, use a quick and efficient post-and-check strategy.

First, invest two to three hours up front in posting your resume to the major job boards, and to a handful of specialty boards. If you're currently employed and looking for a new job, see Chapter Ten for advice on posting your resume confidentially. Some of the best sites to post your resume on include:

- DirectEmployers.com—This is a nonprofit site that offers a collection of job postings from corporate members' Web sites.

- Monster.com

- CareerBuilder.com

- FlipDog.com

- Dice.com (for technical jobs)

- HotJobs.com

- Job boards for your local city or state

- Job boards for your specific career field

- Job boards for military veterans, if you qualify. MilitaryJobs. com and similar sites are among those that work fairly well for job seekers, particularly those in high-tech fields.

Next, pick two days each week to check the boards. Mondays and Thursdays are good, because the new postings from the weekend appear on Monday, and those posted midweek often appear on Thursday. On each of those days, make a quick run through the new job postings and respond to any that look good. Avoid the urge to wander back to the boards on your "off" days, because your hours will be far better spent on your direct-calling campaign.

Respond *only* to ads that exactly match your skills and experience. It may be tempting to apply for a position if your talents are in the ballpark, but it typically won't work. Less than one percent of people who apply for online positions meet the criteria that employers specify, but that's enough to knock you out of the running if you don't have the right credentials.

Also, do not send more than one resume for an advertised position. When you send a resume for a perfect-sounding job and never get a reply, it's hard to resist resending your information in the hopes of getting a second shot at the position. However, it's almost always futile. Instead, wait a week or two for a response and, if you don't get one, add the company to your direct-calling list.

A few additional tips that can save you time, effort, and frustration:

- Keep a list of every job board where you post your resume, as well as the user name and password you use. Then, if you think of an important change you should make, it will be simple to edit or replace a resume you previously posted.

- Preview your resume before you post it. If spelling or grammar is problematic for you, have someone else proof it for you.

- Choose a good title for your resume. For instance, "Technical Writer—Medical Field Expertise" is far better than "Writer."

Create a single generic resume that you can post on multiple job boards. However, when you send a resume in response to a specific post on a job board, consider tweaking it a bit to play up the specific skills and experience being called for in the ad.

Job boards have another important benefit besides listing open positions—they're a great way to evaluate the job market. While you're skimming the boards, get extra value for your effort by using them as a research tool. If a company's name pops up frequently, and particularly if it seems to be hiring managers for new projects, do a little extra research on that firm and see if it's conducting a major hiring push. If so, add it to the list of firms you plan to call directly.

Beware of Job-Board Fraud

If you respond to listings on job boards, never give out any information that can be used to steal your identity. Legitimate job posters never ask for your social security number, marital status, or credit card information. Also, be extra cautious about responding to job postings from entities outside of the United States. In addition, be aware that job boards—including the most major and reputable ones—may sell your personal information (name, address, e-mail address, etc.) to advertisers and other third parties. That's another good reason to limit the number of resumes you post on these boards.

If you are a victim of a fraudulent job board, or are defrauded by someone posing online as a potential employer, report the problem to the Internet Fraud Complaint Center, which is a partnership between the FBI and the National White Collar Crime Center. The agency can be contacted online at *www.ifccfbi.gov.*

Visit Corporate Web Sites

Because job boards are so high profile and advertise themselves so effectively, many people think that online job-hunting begins and ends with Monster, HotJobs, and FlipDog. Job seekers tend to assume that if a company has a job to offer, it'll automatically post that job on the boards. However, that assumption is frequently wrong.

In reality, corporate subscriptions to the major job boards are very costly. A company will pay tens of thousands of dollars to list jobs on these boards, and thousands more to gain access to their resume databases, and many companies don't think they get their money's worth. As a result, most firms forego job board subscriptions when the market is full of eager job seekers, and instead use their corporate Web sites to spread the word about job openings. Because of this, you're as likely to find good leads at a company's Web site as you are by checking the boards.

To maximize your results when you search corporate sites, use the "favorites" pull-down on your web browser to bookmark the employment page of each company you want to track. This makes checking for new listings as easy as clicking your way through the bookmarks. I recommend doing this every Monday and Thursday, so you'll catch all new posts quickly.

Network Wisely

Networking is an excellent technique if your career field is booming, but it has its limits when the number of job seekers equals or outnumbers the number of jobs. It should be number two on your list of good job search techniques, right after direct calling, but don't count on it to find you the "cream of the crop" jobs if you're in a field where such jobs are scarce.

That said, you'll want to devote at least some time to contacting the people most likely to be able to help you. That list should include:

- Former managers and colleagues

- Friends in high places   people with a wide professional and social network

- Former professors, if you are a recent graduate

- Family members

I recommend conducting a networking push up-front, in which you call the top ten or twenty people on your list of contacts—for instance, the former manager who nominated you for Employee of the Year, or the professor who'll remember your excellent work on a big project. Once you exhaust your "A List," don't spend a great deal of additional time trying to get in touch with everyone you've ever known. The farther down the list you go, the more likely it is that you'll simply be spending time schmoozing when you could be spending it on more profitable efforts.

Also, while it's smart to spread the word that you're job-hunting when you attend parties and meetings, don't spend a lot of time seeking out networking events. Odds are, you'll just run into other job seekers trying to expand their networks.

When you talk to contacts, don't simply ask, "Do you know of any job openings?" In addition, find out if they know of any insider information or new developments in your industry. For instance, ask if they've heard of any companies that are expanding or developing new products.

As you are networking, be sure to ask your best contacts if it's okay to use them as references. If they say yes, don't list them on your resume. You'll be invading their privacy if you post their names and phone numbers on job boards, and you'll also be handing your target companies a list of potential competitors for the job you want!

When you do get a job, make sure you continue to cultivate your network (see Chapter Ten). Networking works best as a long-term strategy of building and strengthening ties, not as a "call-only-when-you-need-a-job" strategy. Stay in touch with your most important contacts, even if it's only to drop them a holiday card or send an e-mail occasionally.

Check the Trade Journals

These are often overlooked, but they shouldn't be. There's a trade journal or business publication for just about every field, and these can be a valuable source of both job leads and information. Locate the major journals for your line of work, and check their classified ad listings. Many of these journals or professional associations have electronic job boards, some of which are free and some of which are membership or fee-based. Most importantly, peruse trade journals and their job boards for names of contacts you can add to your direct-calling target list.

Skim the Newspaper Ads

Newspapers dominated the world of job advertising until the mid-nineties, when the Internet revolutionized the process of job-hunting. Today's papers list far fewer good jobs, but the want ads are still worth a little of your time. Some companies find that newspaper ads allow them to tap into all areas of a local market, increasing the diversity of their workforce. Other firms that aren't headquartered in a specific location (for instance, chain stores) use Sunday papers to make sure they attract a wide range of local candidates.

Take a quick run through the Sunday help-wanted ads each week, responding only to any that jump off the page (probably not more than one or two per week). If a firm gives a street address or you can track it down, send a hard copy of your resume in addition to e-mailing it, and mail the hard copy flat in a manila envelope with an individualized cover letter. While you're going through the Sunday paper, be sure to check the business section for any tidbits—news about corporate start-ups or expansions, executive promotions, etc.— that could come in handy during your direct-calling campaigns.

Check with Select Recruiters

When you have some extra time, connect with several recruiting firms that specialize in placing candidates in your line of work. Ask where they've successfully placed candidates with your skills, and how much experience they have. When you find two or three recruiting firms that impress you, send them copies of your resume and stay in touch. There's only a small chance that these recruiters will have an immediate opportunity, but over time they can be a valuable resource—particularly if you take the time to cultivate your relationship with them. Do this even after you get a job, if an agency's recruiters were particularly helpful or courteous during your job search. By sending potential candidates their way as the job market picks up, or giving them a heads-up when your new company is hiring, you'll cement a positive relationship that can help both of you.

Also, get in touch with any recruiters who've successfully placed you in the past, particularly if you had a positive working relationship. Recruiters are more likely to go the extra mile for candidates they know and like.

The One Job-Search Technique to Avoid

"We'll do your job-hunting for you!"

"Our secret network of top-level managers gives you the inside track on hundreds of open jobs."

"We're impressed by your resume, and we can help you get a $100,000-a-year career."

These come-ons can sound like the answer to your prayers, especially if you've spent weeks or months searching for a job with no results. But many career-marketing firms (also known as job search consulting firms) only come with one real guarantee: They'll separate you from a great deal of money.

——— TALE from the TRENCHES ———

The *New York Times* recently told the story of Ian Leicht, who fell for an e-mail he received after five months of job-hunting in Los Angeles. "It said they were in receipt of my credentials and that . . . they had opportunities for me," Leicht says. The firm's representative told Ian he could easily get him a job paying $200,000 a year. The only requirement: He had to pay an up-front fee of $3,600. Leicht put up half the money but received nothing in return except a slightly revamped resume. Karol Phelps went to a similar career management firm in Kansas City, and paid out $5,985. The company promised to introduce her to powerful corporate decision makers, but instead she wound up getting lists of names from newspaper ads, Internet sites, and databases. She told the *Kansas City Star*, "They make you feel they have a secret network of people. But they didn't have any network that could help me."

The typical fee charged by these firms ranges from $3,000 to $6,000, and many firms expect you to pay most or all of that money up front. In return, they promise inside leads on secret jobs, claim that they'll conduct an active job search for you, and sometimes offer vague assurances that when you're hired, the company that hires you will refund that fee. Don't believe any of it.

There are a few legitimate firms in the pay-up-front category, but they cater exclusively to senior executives in the $200,000-a-year salary range, and they charge a very high fee. If you've reached this career level, do your homework and select a career-marketing company with a proven track record. Otherwise, avoid any firm that promises you miracles in exchange for cash up-front.

The world is full of desperate job seekers, and not surprisingly, it's also full of predators willing to take advantage of that desperation. Among them are dozens of pay-up-front career marketing firms that offer the moon, but generally provide clients with nothing more than information that's readily available at the library or on the Internet. Here's good advice: *Never, ever* give your money up-front to any career-marketing agency. This is work you can do yourself. These firms have no magic pill that makes your job search quick and painless.

If you do decide at some point that you're overwhelmed by the effort of job-hunting on your own, there are legitimate firms that will charge you on a "pay as you go" basis to help you with your resume, interview skills, and other aspects of your job search. However, you can get the same help, for a far smaller price tag, by using freelance resume writers (cost: $25 to $50 for a resume makeover), job coaches (cost: between $50 and $100 per hour), or information that's readily available from books or the Internet.

Resume Spamming? Forget It!

Another popular but worthless job-hunting method is "resume spamming," in which you pay somewhere between $40 and $80 to have your resume "blasted" to hundreds or even thousands of companies.

What you get for your money is a resume that looks exactly like spam, and will receive the same treatment.

A spammed resume actually hurts your chances (if it's ever spotted at all), because it tells an employer that you're too lazy to do your own research and to identify companies that can benefit from your skills. Moreover, resume spammers will contribute to the junk e-mail in your own inbox, because these companies will in turn sell your name and e-mail address to other spammers.

The Bottom Line: Effort Equals Payoff

In summary, there's good reason to use some traditional methods such as networking and job boards, but don't rely on them to quickly find you a job that's perfect for you—because they probably won't. Think of them as *low-effort, low-payoff strategies.* They aren't likely to yield the best results, but it won't hurt to invest a few hours a week on them.

Conversely, there's good reason to avoid too-good-to-be-true strategies, such as pay-up-front job-search firms and resume spamming companies. There almost always are *no-effort, no-payoff strategies* that won't accomplish anything except to drain your bank account and your self-esteem.

Now, it's time to turn to the strategy that works: direct calling.

Direct calling is powerful because it's a *maximum effort, maximum payoff* technique. You will work harder at this approach than you've ever worked on a job-hunting campaign—and, as with any other project, the more work you put into it, the more rewards you will earn. You won't be competing with the 10,000 other people who are deluging Intel or Morgan Stanley with their resumes. You won't spend the day gossiping with other job seekers and justify it as "networking." And you won't be going to Monster.com ten times a day to see if somehow, magically, the job you need is there.

Instead, you will make that job happen. How? By changing the rules of the game. Instead of waiting for a miracle, or abdicating control of your job hunt to recruiters or HR staffers or career marketers, you will control every step of your job-search process. And while almost everyone else is surfing Monster or HotJobs, spamming resumes, or seeking help from a dwindling list of networking contacts, you'll be talking directly with the people who control the jobs.

How do you find these people? As you'll see in the next chapter, it's easy—if you're willing to do a little digging.

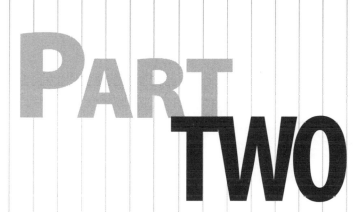

PART TWO

The Fifteen-Day Direct-Calling Campaign:

Your Game Plan for Success

CHAPTER FOUR

Identify Your Targets—
And Know What They Want

Your direct-calling campaign starts not with the telephone but with the Internet, the library, and other places where you'll use intensive "data mining" techniques to locate your target companies and contacts. You'll also uncover key facts about these companies. Who are they? What do they do? What are their strengths and weaknesses? Where are they headed? Who are their customers? What makes them unique? Most importantly, you'll gather clues that allow you to answer the crucial question: What skills/experience/talents do I have that are a perfect match for this company?

Now that you know just how powerful direct calling can be, you're probably tempted to stop reading and start dialing. But don't reach for the phone just yet.

Instead, get ready to do some serious, in-depth detective work. This chapter will tell you how to prepare for your intensive fifteen-day calling campaign by gathering all of the facts, figures, and names you'll need to make your calls count. This step is one of the most crucial *and* most overlooked stages of direct calling, and it's one reason why you'll succeed when most other direct callers won't.

Knowledge Is Power

In any important undertaking, preparation is a crucial part of the job. Lance Armstrong wins the Tour de France time after time not only because he's a great athlete, but also because he spends months training, planning, and reviewing the course before the day of the race. Tom Clancy sells books not only because he's an excellent writer, but also because he and his collaborators do a massive amount of research before they put words to paper.

TALE from the TRENCHES

Between 2000 and 2002, the telecom industry cratered, and millions of people lost their jobs as a result. Scores of companies went out of business. When job opportunities did become available, the competition among job seekers—and among technical recruiters as well—was ferocious. I struggled along with everyone else, but when I spotted an opportunity, I made sure I made the most of it. I researched each firm thoroughly until I was confident that I understood exactly what each company did and what it needed. This up-front research took time and effort, but it paid off handsomely. In one situation, more than 150 candidates were vying for a technical recruiting assignment with a major telecom firm in San Diego. The Vice President of Human Resources hired me for the position, over all of those other candidates, because—as she put it—"You know more about what the company is doing than I do!"

Similarly, you'll take your direct-calling campaign to a higher level by identifying your targets, studying them carefully, and identifying their needs and how you can fill them—well before you reach for the telephone.

The first goal of your research will be to identify the companies you want to reach, and the contacts you're going to call at each of these firms. But that's just the beginning. In addition, you'll mine the Internet and other sources for all of the data you can uncover about each company. With that information in hand, you'll know exactly how to "sell" yourself to each contact when it's time to make your calls.

Research is a step that many job seekers could skip in the past. Companies didn't expect to find perfect matches for their jobs. They didn't mind training an employee who lacked experience, or making allowances for a candidate whose skills were in the ballpark. And they didn't expect you to be an expert on their needs and goals; in fact, they had to worry about *your* needs and goals, in order to attract you.

Now, in today's global economy, many companies can be as picky as they want to be. This means that to score a job, you'll need to prove that you're just the right person to meet an employer's needs. And to do that, you need to know exactly what those needs are.

Where to Start

It's a good bet that you're not a professional detective. That's not a problem, because the resources that you need to locate the contacts you'll approach, and to become an expert on what they want and need, are all at your fingertips. You'll require only a few tools: a computer, Internet access, and online or paper copies of newspapers in your target markets.

With the help of these resources, you'll be able to locate a wealth of data—everything from the names of your target companies' key managers to these firms' annual profits, key products, corporate structure, and future outlook. If you don't have your own computer with Internet access, find a friend or relative who does, or make arrangements to spend time at your local library. You can also check the newspapers while you're at the library (or locate copies at larger bookstores) if you don't have subscriptions.

The data you'll be collecting will accumulate quickly, and you'll need to manage it like professional recruiters do. To do this, you'll want to create two forms that you'll use to record data. One is a worksheet on which you'll record all of the information you'll uncover about each of your target firms. The other is a report that you'll use later to keep track of your contacts when you start your direct-calling campaign.

The Company Research Worksheet

You'll discover, as you begin your detective work, that the amount of information available about many firms on the Internet is mind-boggling. To simplify your search, the most critical categories of information are identified and included in the following chart, the sample Company Research Worksheet. If you know this data, you'll be more prepared than 80 percent of people competing for the jobs you want.

You'll need one of these forms for each firm you plan to contact. It's handiest to create these forms in a spreadsheet or word processing program, so you can update them easily as you find new information, but it's also fine to write out your data by hand in a loose-leaf or spiral notebook.

Company Research Worksheet

Company Name_____

Parent Company, Divisions, or Subsidiaries of Company_____

_____

Location_____

Phone_____

Web Site Address_____

Description of Business_____

Competitors_____

_____

Current Company Projects or Initiatives_____

_____

Hiring Contacts and Titles_____

Position Sought_____

What Can I Bring to This Company?_____

_____

Additional Pertinent Information_____

_____

Some of these categories are self-explanatory, but several require a closer look. Here's an explanation of the data you'll be seeking:

Description of Business

Here, you'll want to answer such questions as: What products does the company make? What services do they provide? How do they make money? Other useful data might include: How long have they been in business? How well are they doing? Are they growing or struggling? What is their annual profit? How many employees do they have?

Competitors

Find out who your target firm's leading rivals are, how well the firm is doing in comparison to those competitors, and any areas in which your target firm excels or is weak in comparison to the competition. Identify the key differences between competitors' products or services and those of your target firm.

Current Company Projects or Initiatives

Here's where you'll want to focus the majority of your efforts, because this is where the keys to the kingdom are likely to reside. That's because the best way to beat out your competition is by being able to answer the deceptively simple question: "What can you tell us about what our company does?" You'd be amazed how many candidates *can't* answer that question.

To be able to name specific current work, or talk in detail about upcoming projects, shows genuine concern for the company, and hiring contacts will take notice. When you combine this information with facts about how your skills relate to specific projects (see the next section), you'll have a formidable presentation.

Here's an illustration of how powerful knowledge about a company's projects can be. Picture yourself in the hiring manager's chair at a software firm, and ask yourself which of these two candidates you'd hire. The first is Bob, who says, "Well, I know that you sell educational software, and that you need Java developers." The second is

Latanya, who says, "I know that you sell educational software, and that you're planning to expand into higher-level software packages for online universities. I think my extensive background as a Java developer, combined with the insight I gained while pursuing my master's at an online university, would be particularly helpful. In using online courseware myself, I spotted a number of flaws in the programs that reduce their usability and reliability, and leave them open to competition by a more user-friendly product." Obviously, you'd lean toward Latanya, who knows both what your products are and how she can help you make them better.

What Can I Bring to This Company?

Here, you'll articulate the reasons why the target company could benefit from your talent, skills, and experience. For example: "I should contact this carpentry company because they're looking for experience in roofing and trusses, and that's one of my areas of expertise." This information will be priceless when you make your initial calls and equally valuable when a contact calls you back. When the latter happens, you'll be able to quickly call up your notes and recite verbatim the reasons why you're a great fit for a particular job. Contacts will be impressed that you already know both the structure of the company *and* what value you can bring to it.

Additional Pertinent Information

Use this to list any facts that enhance your knowledge of the company or its hiring needs. This can include anything from facts about a company's corporate culture and management style to comments made by key personnel in talks or articles. Use your instincts, because sometimes you can parlay a small piece of information into an instant rapport with a contact. For instance, you might be able to get some mileage from the fact that a potential contact served in the same branch of the military as you, or graduated from the same university.

Complete your Company Research Worksheet forms before you start making your calls, so you can focus solely on making calls when you begin your fifteen-day campaign. Make sure that you always know the key facts about a particular company before you call a contact there.

TALE from the TRENCHES

Years ago, Franklin Fullerman, CEO of the marketing firm The Business Champion, was the recruiting manager for a *Fortune* 500 industrial firm. Fullerman's firm strongly preferred to hire candidates from big-name, Ivy League schools. One day, a candidate from a less prestigious school contacted him and wrangled an interview. The young man had studied everything he could find about the financial and operating conditions of the company, and presented an in-depth proposal on how to improve the profitability of its industrial machinery group. Fullerman was so impressed that he hand-carried his resume to the director of the prestigious Executive Training Program.

Still hung up on the idea of an Ivy League staff, the director refused to interview the candidate. Unfazed, the young man called back a few weeks later. He'd done further research and shared his findings with Fullerman. The candidate's analysis was so brilliant that Fullerman insisted that the director interview him. The candidate was hired on the spot.

In addition to getting you a job, careful research can help you avoid wasting time on jobs you don't want. In the course of investigating your target companies, you may read about a company's product and say, "That sounds like another flash-in-the-pan—they'll probably be out of business in a year." Or you'll read about a company's corporate culture and realize that if you did get hired, you'd be a square peg in a round hole. (For instance, one manager, a happy couch potato, decided not to waste time applying to a company run by a fitness fanatic who regularly took his staff on mountain climbs.) Job-hunting is an ordeal, and there's no point in adding to that ordeal by wasting your time on companies who aren't a good match for your skills, interests, lifestyle, and personality.

To summarize, you have three goals in this stage:

- To compile all of the key facts you need to know about your target companies.

- To determine where these companies' needs and your skills intersect.

- To determine which companies are a good fit for you and which are not.

Once you've accomplished these goals, you're ready to move on to the next step: preparing to track the results of your direct-calling campaign.

The Hiring Contact Status Report

After you've completed the entries in your Company Research Worksheet, there's still one more form you'll need to build: a Hiring Contact Status Report form similar to the one shown below. You'll use

GET hired FAST!

this form every day during your calling campaign to quickly access the phone numbers you need, and to record the results of your calls. Use the blank columns to enter in data as you gather more research and make your calls.

Hiring Contact Status Report

Hiring Contact Title Company	Office phone Alternate or mobile phone Hiring contact e-mail	Attempted call date, results and next steps

Where Do You Find Contacts?

Now you're ready to begin your homework. Your goal is to identify at least 150 contacts if possible, and obtain information about how to reach and impress them. It's not necessary for all of these contacts to be at different firms (in fact, you may have several at a single large firm), but do your best to achieve this goal.

Finding this many influential contacts may sound impossible, but realize that direct calling isn't like networking, because you don't need to know these contacts personally. You just need to *want* to know them.

How do you find these people? It's simpler than you'd think. It's also fairly easy to mine the Internet for data about their respective companies, although it will take you several days of intensive work. Don't skip this stage, because it's absolutely crucial to making your fifteen-day "big push" successful.

Not an Expert "Internet Miner"? No Problem

If you're experienced at surfing the Internet and uncovering online information, you can skip this section. If not, the next few paragraphs will give you all the information you'll need in order to master basic online research. There's no reason to be intimidated by the Internet, because you'll find that "Internet mining" is easy to do if you know a few search tricks.

To start, go to Google *(www.google.com)*. There are dozens of major search engines, but Google is a good place to start, because it's one of the best. The search techniques that work on Google will work on most other search engines, although you'll want to check each engine's instructions to make sure. Below, we'll list the rules used by Google, with some notes about different rules used by other search engines.

To search for information on a company, you'll type keywords in the search box. This is simple, if you know the basic rules of search grammar. They are:

1. To perform a Google search for a Web site that includes ALL of your search terms, simply list the words (e.g., electroplating Cleveland). Some search engines may require you to include an "AND" between the words, or a + sign, if you require that a keyword be included in the results (e.g., +elvis +impersonators).

   The more terms you include, the more specific your search will be—so add keywords if you're overwhelmed by too many returns, and delete keywords if you've made your search too restrictive and don't turn up any results.

2. To search for either of two words, use OR. For instance, if you aren't sure whether you should search using the keyword banking or the keyword financial, simply say banking OR financial.

3. To search for a phrase, put it in quotes (e.g., "medical technical writing"). This will ensure that the search engine looks for the entire phrase, and not just each individual word.

4. Some search engines allow you to use the term NEAR to find pages where two words occur close together. For instance, typing airbags NEAR manufacturing on AltaVista will turn up Web pages in which those two words occur within ten words of each other.

Need more assistance? You can find plenty of additional tips on Internet searching by going to Google and typing in "search engine tutorial."

Best Bets for Corporate Information on the Net

How easy it will be to find the data you're seeking will vary depending on a variety of factors, including how large or small your target companies are, how influential they are, and whether they're public or privately held. In some cases, you'll be able to fill in all the blanks on your Company Research Worksheet simply by checking one or two sites. Other times, you'll need to dig a little deeper.

The depth of your search will also depend on how keenly you want to work for each firm. Your top five or ten target firms should rate an intensive search, while the basic information on the Company Research Worksheet is adequate for less desirable firms.

Among the sources you can use to obtain information are:

Search engines

Go to Google, Yahoo, or other large search engines, and type in the names of the companies you're researching. Also try searching on the names of company CEOs. Most likely, you'll find valuable articles that mention other key personnel. If these people sound like good contacts, run secondary searches on their names as well. Don't hesitate to do some burrowing, because it can lead you to contacts you otherwise wouldn't find.

You can also use search engines to find newspaper and/or magazine articles that discuss your target companies' strengths, weaknesses, past history, and future prospects. Often these articles are a far better source of critical and unbiased information than the companies' own Web sites.

Company Web sites

When you go to each firm's Web site, look for any mentions of department heads or other key employees. Also look to see if there's an online copy of the company's newsletter (a good source of names), or a "press releases" section, which is likely to mention the names of potential contacts. If the company's annual report is available on its Web site, scan it and analyze how well the company is doing, what its future plans are, who owns the company, and who its chief executives are. Look for information about what the company does, how many people it employs, and what its culture is like.

Hoover's Online—www.hoovers.com

Some of the data on this site is available only to subscribers, but you'll find a goldmine of free facts about large companies and many smaller ones. For instance, Hoover's lists the names of each firm's major corporate executives, annual sales and growth figures, and information about each company's industry and chief competitors. In addition, click on the "news" section for each company, which is an outstanding source of up-to-date information.

Vault—www.vault.com

Like Hoover's, this subscription-based site offers information— some of it free— about the revenues, leadership, and products of each company. In addition, its "company snapshots" give you an inside look at the corporate culture of each firm—both good points and bad. Also check the "gold surveys" and "messages" sections, where you'll learn what employees of each listed company think about its prospects, culture, and products.

IndustryWeek—www.industryweek.com

This site offers free information on the top 1,000 manufacturing companies internationally and the top 500 in the United States, as well as news on industry trends.

Bizjournals—www.bizjournals.com

You can subscribe free of charge at this site to read current and archived articles from your local city's business journal, and to sign up for e-mailed news updates.

The Annual Report Gallery—www.reportgallery.com

This site links to more than 2,000 annual reports from large and midsized companies.

Yahoo Corporate Reports   http://finance.yahoo.com

This site offers extensive, free information about corporations, as well as the latest news reports and data on competing firms and industry-wide trends.

CorporateInformation.com— www.corporateinformation.com

This site requires free registration; it allows you to research hundreds of companies, both in the U.S. and abroad.

The Industry Research Desk—http://virtualpet.com/industry/howto/search.htm

This site offers links to more than thirty different U.S. and international industry portals. Check out the page on "How to Learn

GET hired FAST!

About an Industry or a Specific Company," for additional links to valuable sites.

Gateway to Associations Online—http://info.asaenet.org/gateway/OnlineAssocSlist.html

Enter keywords for your field, and check each association listing to see if it includes member directories that can provide you with contacts. You'll find other key facts as well; for instance, a search on "physics" will lead you to the American Institute of Physics, which offers state-by-state listings of companies that have recently hired graduates with bachelor's degrees in physics.

Give.org—www.give.org

This site is an outstanding source of information on nonprofit organizations. Go to "charity reports" and click on any organization's name to obtain information including primary projects, budget, staff size, and CEO name. The amount of information available depends on what is provided by each charity, but larger and more reputable nonprofits generally list a wealth of data.

Guidestar—www.guidestar.org

Here's another good source of information on nonprofits. While some information is for paid subscribers only, basic information is free.

Local newspapers

In these, you'll find information about mergers, acquisitions, new products, expansions and layoffs, profit statements, and new company start-ups.

Business Wire—www.businesswire.com

At this site you'll find a free, comprehensive listing of news releases from thousands of national and international companies and organizations.

Web sites of civic groups or clubs

The more prestigious civic clubs are often heavily populated by corporate executives, and sometimes you can locate contact information about them (e.g., business phone numbers or e-mail addresses) that isn't listed on a corporate Web site.

Web sites listing industry conferences

Every industry spawns associations, and those associations have frequent conferences featuring company leaders. Using the Web sites created to publicize these conferences, you can often track down important contacts. Simply enter your specialty as a search term, and then the word "association" or "conference" (for instance, ASIC and conference).

Corporate alumni Web sites

These sites, which allow former employees of companies to stay in contact, can be a great way to find old friends and colleagues during the networking phase of your job-hunt. More importantly, they can steer you to important new contacts in high-level positions at your target companies. The site for Digital Equipment Corporation alumni, for instance, lists the names of hundreds of former DEC employees—many of whom are now CEOs, VPs, directors, or managers at their new companies.

By combining some or all of these sources, you should have no trouble locating critical data and finding hiring contacts at your target companies. If you need additional help, a reference librarian can steer you to more online and offline resources.

Now Comes the Hard Part

Once you're done filling in your Company Research Worksheet, and you've located all of the necessary contact numbers for your Hiring Contact Status Report, the initial research phase of your job hunt will be completed. You'll have the names and phone numbers you need, you'll be prepared to speak knowledgeably and confidently over any contact you reach, and you'll be able to demonstrate your superiority over other candidates competing for the job you want. At this point, you're set to tackle the action phase of your plan: translating the wealth of information you've accumulated into successful contacts, job interviews, and, eventually, a great job offer.

Are you ready for one of the biggest challenges of your life? If so, it's time to get started. In the next chapter, you'll learn exactly how you can use the information you've just gathered in order to "sell" yourself to the people who can put you to work.

CHAPTER FIVE

Making Contact: Your Fifteen-Day Action Plan

Three interviews in three weeks, and, in the end, a brand-new job—all through your own efforts. Sound impossible? Not if you have what it takes to tackle the ambitious campaign outlined in this chapter. You'll learn how to reach the people who make hiring decisions, how to develop fail-safe "scripts" for any situation that may arise when you make your calls, and how to convince hiring managers that you're the ideal candidate for their jobs.

This is the step that will land you a new or better job—and it's the step that takes pure, raw courage. There's no way to sugarcoat it. What you are about to do will be awkward, painful, sometimes embarrassing, and above all, difficult. It will test your strength and your resolve. But the payoff is huge. If you follow the instructions in this chapter to the letter, your hard work will bring you face-to-face with the people who need you. It will make you a front-runner for the "invisible" jobs that aren't posted on Monster or CareerBuilder, and it will place you light years ahead of people who limit their efforts to networking, mailing resumes, and responding to postings on job boards.

A recent *New York Times* poll shows that 72 percent of job seekers who've grown frustrated with traditional job-search methods are now using the direct-call technique. If you don't join them, you could be dooming yourself to a long, frustrating, and ultimately failed job search. If you do follow their lead, you'll virtually guarantee that you'll score one or more job interviews within a month.

To Succeed, You Need to Do It Right

Direct calling is incredibly effective, but it isn't easy. In fact, it's one of the hardest things you'll ever do. It's amazing how many experts tell job seekers to use the direct-calling technique without telling them exactly how it's done. That's like handing a sixteen-year-old the keys to the car and saying, "Here's the ignition switch—just figure out the rest by yourself." Doing direct calling without proper preparation can be a recipe for failure.

Direct calling is an advanced job-hunting skill, and the only way to make it work is to do it *exactly right*. When you do, you'll virtually eliminate competition from other candidates, including those who use the direct calling method without knowing how to succeed at it. Success lies not just in calling the key people who control hiring, but in impressing them—and impressing them fast.

That's why this chapter will arm you with every tool you'll need to quickly convince a hiring manager that you're better than your competitors. In the following pages, you'll find reports, charts, and scripts that will enable you to perfect your direct-calling technique. Like a movie star who prepares for a role, you'll know exactly how to hit your mark, say the right lines, and grab your audience, and how to keep improving your performance until it's flawless.

That doesn't mean that every call (or even most of your calls) will be a success. Far from it! Remember the success ratio we discussed earlier. In times when the job market is at its worst, you can expect:

50 calls to lead to
8 connections, which lead to
1 interview

At times when the market is at its best, you can expect:

25 calls to lead to
4 connections, which lead to
1 interview

These numbers continually fluctuate as the job market changes, but be assured that you will hear negative responses far more than you'll hear positive ones. In fact, you are about to encounter an enormous amount of rejection, and you'll undergo three of the most challenging weeks of your life. The good news is that if you have the courage to accept this challenge, at some point you will finally hear a "yes"—and probably more than one.

Moreover, by accepting this challenge, you'll put yourself in control of your job search. You'll replace endless waiting and self-doubt with a proven game plan, and replace inaction with forward motion. When you're finally fed up with unsuccessful networking, resumes that disappear into black holes, and job boards that don't produce results, you'll find it amazingly liberating to say, "I'm taking charge."

This approach can land you a job if you don't have one, and it can also get you a better job if you're currently working but dissatisfied with your circumstances. The best time to find a job is when you have one. Hiring managers are impressed by individuals who take the initiative in improving their careers—which is what you'll be doing when you call them directly.

One last warning, however: When you undertake this plan, be prepared to commit a great deal of time, energy, and emotional resources to it. This is not a plan for the faint of heart. It won't work if you do it casually or haphazardly. And it won't work if you say, "I like this step and I'll do it, but I'll skip this other step because it's too hard/too boring/too tedious." To guarantee your success, follow these steps religiously, and don't quit even when it gets hard—and it will. In the end, your payoff will be well worth every bit of your effort and pain.

Are you ready to trade easy but failed approaches for a tough approach that will get you results? If so, here's the eight-step program for what you need to do.

Step 1: Assemble Your Tools

In the last chapter, you created two forms: a Company Research Worksheet, and a Hiring Contact Status Report. These tools will be critical to your success, and now it's time to put them to use.

Your Company Research Worksheet contains all of the data you assembled about each contact you plan to make. At this stage, you'll use your data to become an expert on each company you plan to approach. In the process, you'll elevate your direct-calling campaign to a professional level by laying a solid foundation for your calls in the same way professional recruiters do.

Before each call, review every fact you've uncovered about the firm you'll be contacting. As you do this, ask yourself: How do my skills match this company's needs? Why would they pick me out of a crowd? Is there something unique I can offer them? For instance: Did an online magazine mention that the furniture company that's offering the sales job you want is enhancing its services by offering free interior decorating advice to clients? If so, mention that in addition to sales experience, you have an associate's degree in interior design. Did the firm's Web site list numerous clients in Mexico? If so, make a note to mention that you're fluent in Spanish. Be absolutely fanatical about this step, because you need to be supremely confident both about your knowledge of each target company, and about what you can bring to the table.

Your Hiring Contact Status Report is equally crucial. Once you start calling, you'll need to update this chart after each call you make. Do this step religiously, because you will be compiling a huge amount of data over the next three weeks, and you don't want to risk losing it by using a disorganized system. When a hiring contact calls back, you'll need to be able to pull up your notes quickly and feel confident that they're accurate. Few things are more embarrassing than getting a call-back and failing to remember why you called the person, the message you left, or what you previously spoke about. Conversely, you'll make an excellent impression if you remember important facts and details.

Step 2: Set Your Goals

Based on the data collected by many corporate and technical recruiters, here is your realistic target for your fifteen-day plan:

You will succeed in getting three interviews in three weeks.

That's an ambitious goal in today's job market, if you're in a field that's not in high demand. Many recruiters know outstanding individuals who've diligently networked and sent out resumes for months without getting a single nibble. But if you're willing to make obtaining a new job your top priority, and you follow this plan to the letter, you'll succeed in scoring your interviews, whether you're a new college graduate, a midlevel professional, or a senior executive.

The first key to reaching your goal of three interviews in three weeks is to set and accomplish a tough set of daily goals. Do NOT deviate from these goals, no matter how hard the going gets. Here are the targets you need to make:

Job Search Goal: To Set Up Three Interviews in Three Weeks

Note: these goals are based on a difficult job market. If hiring is good in your field, you may easily exceed these targets.

Job Search Schedule for the Next Fifteen Days:

Mondays and Fridays:

- Five calls to hiring contacts in the morning

- Five calls to hiring contacts in the afternoon

- Arrange or complete one in-depth phone conversation with hiring contact within a selected company

Tuesdays, Wednesdays, and Thursdays:

- Five calls to hiring contacts in the morning

- Five calls to hiring contacts in the afternoon

- Arrange or complete two in-depth phone conversations with hiring contacts within a selected company

Target by end of fifteen days:

- 150 calls to hiring contacts

- Twenty-four in-depth phone conversations with hiring contacts

- Three personal interviews

What If It Doesn't Work?

The odds of this approach letting you down are remote. Statistics predict that your conversations will translate into three onsite interviews (and perhaps four or five). But what if you prove to be a statistical anomaly? Be assured that your research and calls won't be in vain. Thanks to your hard work, you'll have built a second tier of hiring contacts. If you're professional during your initial calls, contacts will frequently respond by referring you to colleagues who might have job openings. In all likelihood, this secondary list will include forty to fifty people. You'll be in an even stronger position when you call these new contacts, because you were referred by someone they know and trust. So if the statistics don't play out like they should at first, simply move on to Round Two of your calls.

Making as many as 150 calls does not necessarily mean that you'll contact 150 different companies. It could mean calling five people in each of thirty different companies, or ten people in fifteen companies, or so on, depending on the size and diversity of business units in your target firms.

Your purpose, quite simply, will be to connect with hiring contacts at the companies of your choosing—whether there are five, fifty, or 150 companies on your list. And your short-term goal will be equally simple: to speak with one to two hiring contacts per day, whether these people are corporate recruiters, human resources managers, directors of a department, hiring managers in your job specialty, or any other individuals who can bring you one step closer to getting a job.

Remember that you are playing the odds, and the odds are in your favor because you're going to make a very large number of calls. This is one of the chief reasons you'll even beat out competitors who use direct calling, because most of them will make only a handful of connections. This means that your chances of getting a job are significantly higher than theirs—even though they're using the same technique.

Step 3: Get Your Game Face On

Direct calling requires confidence, but the very newness of this job-hunting strategy can be daunting. Calling a hiring manager out of the blue and asking him or her to consider you as a candidate violates the unwritten rules of job-hunting. As a result, your first impulse may be, "I can't do this!" Many people throw their hands up and exclaim, "Forget it! I'm not a salesperson."

In reality, however, you're an expert at influencing other people, because you do it every day. Think of the last few times you've convinced people to do things they weren't interested in doing. Did you talk your last employer into letting you take on a new project, convince your friends to try a new restaurant, or persuade your City Council to change a zoning law? If so, you know how to influence people. This chapter will teach you how to take this skill to a new level.

You'll feel more confident about doing this when you realize that when you contact hiring managers, you won't be doing what marketers and recruiters call "cold calling"—the approach that the vast majority of direct-calling job seekers use. In cold calling, the caller knows virtually nothing about the contact. It's a good way to waste people's time, but not a good way to impress them. Instead, thanks to the detective work you did in Chapter Four, you'll know exactly who your targets are, and exactly why they should want you.

It's important to have confidence in your ability to persuade people—and to have confidence in yourself as well. The global job market has changed so radically over recent years that many of the "best and brightest" are either unemployed or working at unsatisfactory jobs (see Chapter One). If you're one of them, there's nothing wrong with you or your job skills. What's wrong are the old-school job-search techniques that aren't helping you get hired—and now you're retooling and refocusing on a solution that will get the results you need.

Step 4: Plan Your Timing

A key, but often overlooked, component of calling a hiring contact is the time of day. The people you're attempting to reach are doing more work today, with fewer resources, than ever before. Fifty- to sixty-hour workweeks aren't uncommon among hiring managers and other potential contacts, and interrupting a key contact at the wrong time doesn't help your chances.

That's why you will want to schedule your calls for the following times:

- 6:30 to 8 A.M., before the workday starts
- 5:00 to 7:00 P.M., after the workday ends

Another key time to reach people is during the day at fifty minutes past the hour. This is an optimum time because contacts typically come out of meetings just before the end of the hour, and head back to their offices to check their e-mail and voice messages. Usually it's a good time to catch them while they have a few minutes between commitments.

Step 5: Rehearse Your Script

Each time you reach a contact you'll have about twenty-five seconds to generate interest, and you'll need to make every second count. Most callers have no idea how to do this. More often than not corporate recruiters and hiring managers spend their days fielding calls from people who approach direct calling by saying, "Hello—I was wondering if you've filled that position listed on your Web site," or simply, "Do you have any openings?" That approach will not garner interest from the people on the other end of the phone. They don't know who you are or, most importantly, what you can do for them. You've only made one impression: that YOU want something (a job) from them. Most likely the response to this approach will be, "Send me a resume and we'll get back to you if we have an interest." That will be the end of the conversation.

A few callers take the next logical step, saying, for instance, "I'm a degreed RF engineer with five years of design experience in two-way communications." The hiring manager will respond, "That's great," and then most likely ask, "What can you tell me about the work we're doing here, and how you could help us?" In many cases, job seekers won't have specific information about the company's projects. They've simply spotted the position on a Web site and want to know if it is filled before sending a resume. Again, they'll probably receive the standard response: "Thanks, send us your resume, and we'll get back to you if we have an interest."

Only rarely do candidates take the time to research a firm's specific projects and identify where the company's needs mesh with their skills. Recruiters know that candidates who do that level of homework up front are likely to be persistent, smart, and goal-oriented. In these cases, the candidate's chances of being sent directly to a hiring manager for an in-depth phone interview increase exponentially. Positions can be difficult to fill in any economy, and when recruiters identify the right skill set and fit, they waste no time in moving on to the next step. This is true, too, for hiring managers.

The moral? Obviously, it's natural to think about your own needs. Right now, for instance, you're more likely to be interested in getting a paycheck to cover your rent or mortgage than in improving the long-term stock price of XYZ Corp. But when you're calling a prospective employer, *it's not about you—it's all about them.* Never forget that the primary tenet of the hiring process is that in order to interest employers in hiring you, you need to give them a reason to want you. That reason isn't your mortgage payment or your rent check. It's your ability to improve their product, their service, or their profits.

That's why, before you make a call, you need to develop a script that will allow you to explain persuasively, in just seconds, how you will make life better for the person at the other end of the phone. The following pages offer a powerful sample script that will enable you to do this. The script includes sample answers in parentheses, based on a script for a wireless project manager. Use the following script as a guide. Simply substitute your own information for the answers in parentheses, aiming for a short but concise script. (Remember those twenty-five seconds!)

This script enables you to quickly:

- Impress your contact with your skills

- Summarize your experience

- Reveal your knowledge of the target company's needs

- Show how your talents fit these needs

Later, after you've developed your basic script, you'll need to tailor it to each individual company and contact you plan to call. It's a lot of work, but it's what makes direct calling effective—and it's why you'll get the job, while somebody who's less prepared won't.

Keep two additional points in mind as you compose your script. The first is: Be honest. Play up your real accomplishments, without embellishing them. The second is: Less is more. There's a limit to how much a listener can absorb all at once, so keep your script focused on a few key points. You can write down a list of secondary points to work into the conversation later.

Your script outline

This basic format covers all of the key points you'll need to make during your calls, in order to impress your contacts quickly.

Hi ___(Jeff)___, I'm ___(Jane Wilson)___, a ___(Project Manager)___ with experience in ___(wireless infrastructure deployment)___ for ___(GSM customers)___ where I've worked for ___(Lucent and Nortel)___.

I know you have ___(a current project with AT&T Wireless)___ for ___(GSM system deployments in the western US)___.

Based on the experience I've had in ____(GSM deployments)____ in ___(Arizona and California)___, I feel I could help your company in this area of work. Would you be interested in talking with me about my background and the work I've done?

Once you've refined your script, you're ready to start rehearsing. Read the script out loud until you feel comfortable and confident and can nearly recite the words from memory. If you find yourself stumbling over any section of the script, see if you can reword that part to sound more natural.

Some people feel awkward or silly scripting out a conversation and rehearsing it like an actor, but keep in mind that a script is simply a tool to enable you to achieve a desired result. In the movie *Jerry Maguire*, did Cuba Gooding, Jr. simply improvise the line, "Show me the money!" as the cameras rolled? No—and yet the line sounded both powerful and perfectly spontaneous. Your goal, similarly, is to prepare yourself to say the most powerful and convincing words you can say, at exactly the right moment. Having your script at hand, and feeling familiar and easy with it, will allow you to do that. And on those occasions when you make it past the twenty-five-second mark and your contact says "Tell me more," you can relax and let the conversation go where it will. By that point, you'll know you've already made your most influential points.

Step 6: Pick Up the Phone

At this point you have every tool you need to succeed at direct calling. Now it's time to start making your calls. Set aside two blocks of time, one in the morning, and one in the evening, on fifteen consecutive weekdays. Sticking to this intense schedule will earn you a new job in the shortest possible time, and having a deadline will keep you highly motivated. If you already have a job and are seeking a better one, adapt this timetable to meet your needs, but schedule five calls per each direct-calling session.

Before beginning your campaign, clear your schedule of any commitments that could interfere with your calling goals. Let other people know that you will be devoting yourself exclusively to your job hunt during the times you designate, and ask them not to interrupt you unless there's an emergency.

Each day, strive to make all of the calls outlined in your goals— no matter how frustrated you become, and no matter how much you want to quit. It's better to begin with a few of your less-desired targets, rather than with the companies you're most interested in working for. This will give you a chance to practice your script, work out any kinks, and become more relaxed with the process of direct calling.

Before you make each call, review the script you've tailored for the firm you'll be contacting, as well as all of the information you've uncovered about that firm. Keep your Company Research Worksheet at hand, in case you need to refer to it during your conversation. Also keep your Hiring Contact Status Report within reach, so that immediately after getting off the phone you can jot down your notes about how the call went.

Once you start making your calls, you'll soon discover that it isn't as scary as it seems. The preparation you've done will eliminate much of your anxiety, and your confidence will be obvious to your contacts because you'll know exactly what you want to say. Speak clearly, and avoid rushing through your script. Also be prepared to adapt to different responses, because even though you've prepped as carefully as you can, it's impossible to know in advance what will happen each time you make a call. In the best-case scenarios, you'll connect directly with the person you want to reach, the two of you will hit it off, and the individual will be very interested in you. This could result in getting an offer for a phone interview or even a face-to-face meeting. Many of your calls, however, will result in less positive responses, and how you handle these responses can make the difference between losing an opportunity and getting a second shot at success.

The following are the most common scenarios you'll encounter, along with the most effective ways to handle them. Review these responses so you'll be familiar with them. Many candidates who don't initially reach their desired contacts still earn a call back or even an interview, because they know how to finesse these situations.

Scenario #1: You call and it rolls into voice mail

Leave the same scripted message you made for your phone call. You'll be consistent, and you won't have to wonder what message you left if the contact calls back. Here's an example:

> "I'm John Smith, a technical recruiter with experience recruiting business development executives for DoD and Homeland Security contractors such as Titan Corporation and ViaSat. I know you're involved in several projects in secured communications for the tactical military radio business of your company. Based on the work you're doing, and the companies I've recruited for in this area, I'd like to ask if I could help you staff the projects you're working on."

At the end of your message, say:

> "Thanks for your consideration and I look forward to hearing from you if my message is of interest. In the event you're in meetings

or traveling and you don't have the opportunity to get back with me, I'll try again in a few days. My number is ___-___-___. Thanks for your time."

Remember that your hiring contact could be in the room, but meeting with someone and not able to pick up the phone. Sound professional and don't just hang up, especially since caller ID will identify you.

Scenario #2: You leave a voice mail message and no one responds

A good voice mail message frequently will get a response. However, if you don't receive a reply in a few days, call again and leave another message. Here's an example:

> "Hi Bill, it's John Smith following up on a call I placed to you a few days ago. I'm the technical recruiter with experience in business development recruiting for two of your closest competitors. In the event you're traveling or away, I wanted to leave another message to let you know I'm interested in talking with you about helping you to staff for the 120 million dollar contract you recently won for secured two-way tactical communications for the Department of Defense. If you have an opportunity I'd enjoy the chance to talk with you. My number is ___-___-___. Thanks and I look forward to hearing from you."

If your contact doesn't respond this time, the individual is probably very busy or not very interested. But if you're really keen on working for this company, leave a final message. Here's an example:

> "Hi Bill, I wanted to try one more time to connect with you, this is John Smith, the technical recruiter with business development

recruiting experience in the DoD and homeland security sectors. I know you're swamped, but in the future, if you have need for someone with my background, hang on to my contact information and give me a call. If it is easier for you to send an e-mail you can do that at john@johnsmithco.com. Thanks for your consideration and I appreciate your time. My number is ___-___-___."

It's best to adopt a "Three Tries and Stop" strategy. If you leave three messages and get no response, it's time to move on to your next hiring contact. A few months down the road you can revisit this hiring contact, but not now. This is very much a numbers game, so don't waste precious time on a single opportunity that might not exist, when there are plenty of others to pursue.

Scenario #3: The secretary answers the phone

Many people tend to freeze up when this happens for fear of being chastised for wanting to talk with an executive or hiring contact. Don't hang up! Administrative people have a very difficult task, which is to shield executives or hiring contacts from people intruding on their time, while making sure that valuable information reaches their bosses. Here's how you make the most of this situation:

"If you have a moment, I need your direction on a question I have. My name is John Smith, and I'm a technical recruiter with experience recruiting senior level business development executives for DoD and Homeland Security contractors such as Titan Corporation and ViaSat. I know your company is involved in several projects in the tactical military radio business. I'd like to ask if you if [hiring contact name] is staffing up for the upcoming work I've read about . . ."

In response to your request, you'll probably be told one of the following three things:

(a). "Send me your resume."

To which you'll respond: "Great—shall I e-mail or fax it to you?" and take it from there.

Or (b). "We're not hiring."

To which you'll reply, "That's understandable. If it's OK with you, I'd like to forward you my resume for future consideration, so when you need someone like me you'll have my credentials handy and we can connect."

All good administrative people are on the lookout for talent for the people they support. Respect what they say, and you increase the likelihood of creating an alliance with them. It's likely that if the right administrative person comes across the right resume at the right time, a connection will be made. You need to increase your odds of this occurring by working with administrative support, not against them. If you succeed, and the administrative person forwards your resume to a senior executive or hiring contact, it'll be read and acted on if there is a need. Otherwise, questions could be asked as to why no action was taken. Believe it—it happens all the time.

(c). "Talk to HR."

To which you'll reply, "I'll be happy to. . . . Is there a recruiter or HR person supporting your group to whom you feel I should speak?" and take it from there. Getting a referral from someone inside a company to talk with someone else inside that company is quite valuable. Thank the administrative person for his or her help, and move on.

Lastly, as your exchange with the administrative person concludes, there are two important questions to ask in closing.

The first is:

> "May I call (hiring contact name) from time to time to see if projects have been added or to see if any new hiring needs arise?"

The second is:

> "What other groups or divisions should I consider within [company name] to see if there may be a fit for my experience?"

Above all, be unfailingly courteous and respectful to the person who answers the phone, whether it's your intended contact or an assistant (and whether they are polite to you or not). Keep in mind that many a job opportunity is made or lost in a conversation with an administrative assistant.

Step 7: Measure Your Progress

After each call, pull up your Hiring Status Contact Report and record the results of your call. It's very important to do this while the call is still fresh in your mind, so you don't forget any important details. At the end of each day, set aside half an hour to review your ten attempted contacts, analyze your successes and difficulties, and plan for the next day. For instance, if a call went very well, try to remember the points you made. If your remarks impressed one manager, they're likely to impress others. If a call went poorly, on the other hand, see if you can determine why—while remembering that the vast majority of your calls will not yield fruit, for reasons that have little to do with you. Here is a form you can use to summarize your results:

Daily Plan and Review

Effectiveness in Connecting with Hiring Contacts:

Successes_____

_____

Weaknesses_____

_____

Ideas for Improving Script_____

_____

Company Research and Hiring Contact name generation_____

_____

Follow Up and Return Call Planning for next day_____

_____

Effectiveness in Talking with Hiring Contacts:

Successes in generating interest during first contact_____

_____

Weaknesses in generating interest during first contact_____

_____

Successes in converting initial conversation to a phone interview_____

_____

Weaknesses in converting initial conversation to a phone interview_____

_____

During this half hour, also pull up your Hiring Contact Status Report, and fill in any comments you didn't enter right after making your calls. Here is an example of what the form you created back in Chapter Four will look like after a day of calling:

Hiring Contact Status Report: Day 1

HIRING CONTACT title company	OFFICE PHONE alternate or mobile phone hiring contact e-mail	RESULTS attempted call date results and next steps
Lee Jones Technical Recruiter Satellite Co.	703-555-1212 n/a abc@def.com	5.12.05: left message to call back, not available to talk, call tomorrow. Company has extensive project underway that matches my business development experience.
Jon Lee VP Bus. Dev. Terrestrial Phone Co.	858-555-1212 n/a ghi@jkl.com	5.12.05: talked with Jon's secretary, she told me Jon is traveling and back next week. I asked to leave voice mail, she put me through. Left introductory message and will follow up next week.
Steve Doe Executive VP Bus. Affairs Jupiter II, Inc.	847-555-1212 n/a mno@pqr.com	5.12.05: called in and got Steve coming out of a meeting, I gave brief introduction and he asked that I call him back later in the day. He liked the experience I had in business development.
Paul Doman Dir. Global Markets NetSat	302-555-1212 n/a n/a	5.12.05: called and went straight to voice mail, left message. I will follow up tomorrow if I don't hear back from him today. Potential good fit based on open position spotted on Monster.com
Chris Orbo Dir. Bus. Dev. Telecomsat	973-555-1212 n/a stu@vwx.com	5.12.05: called in and got Chris on third ring. I gave intro, he liked what I said and we've scheduled a longer call for next Friday. He told me areas of focus they have and said we'd discuss further.

Next, pull up your Job Search Goal list and carry over any follow-up to the next day. Here's a sample form showing one job seeker's results for her overall three-week campaign. Notice that on Days Two and Fourteen, when she missed two calls due to a minor life crisis, she moved those calls to the following days. This is the best way to force yourself to face those ten calls each day—because you'll know that if you don't, the next day will be even harder. Think of it as "tough love."

Job Search Summary Report

	Attempted Calls to Hiring Contacts	Calls Resulting in Phone Conversations with Hiring Contacts	Calls Resulting in Onsite Interviews with Hiring Contacts
Day One	10	2	0
Day Two	8	2	0
Day Three	12	3	0
Day Four	10	2	0
Day Five	10	2	1
Week One Totals	**50**	**11**	**1**
Day Six	10	2	0
Day Seven	12	2	0
Day Eight	12	3	1
Day Nine	12	3	0
Day Ten	4	2	0
Week Two Totals	**50**	**12**	**1**
Day Eleven	10	3	1
Day Twelve	10	2	0
Day Thirteen	10	2	0
Day Fourteen	8	3	1
Day Fifteen	12	2	0
Week Three Totals	**50**	**12**	**2**
GRAND TOTALS	***150***	***35***	***4***

Never let a day go by without analyzing your results and updating your forms. All of this paperwork can be annoying, especially after a stressful day of making calls, but it's a key element of your job search. You'll be spending about 20 percent of your time actually talking with hiring contacts, and the remaining 80 percent in preparation, accurate recording of your data, and subsequent follow-up. The data you'll collect during this process will be priceless, both now and in the future when you need to job-hunt again, so be sure not to skimp on it. Professional recruiters invest thousands of dollars in software programs to track their data, simply because they know that any one phone number, e-mail address, or comment could prove to be crucial a day, a week, a month, or even a year later.

Step 8: Stay Motivated

It's difficult to hear nothing but "no" all day, and it's even harder on days when the people on the other end of the phone go out of their way to be brusque or rude. No amount of psyching up will fully prepare you to handle so much rejection so many times a day, and there is a natural tendency to take it personally. But don't—because it has nothing to do with you, and everything to do with factors that are beyond your control.

To help maintain your motivation in the face of this rejection, keep this analogy in mind: Like a fisherman casting a line, you'll pull up an empty hook dozens of times before you land a prize catch. But your "fish" are out there—and you will catch them, as long as you're persistent enough to keep trying.

An equally motivating aspect of the campaign you are undertaking is that while it's difficult, it is of finite duration (three weeks) and has clearly defined goals (ten hiring contacts per day for fifteen days).

You have a specific focus, plan, and mission, and you have an outstanding chance of having an offer on the table within a month. In short, while this phase is the toughest, and may even seem impossible on some days, it will end soon—and it's virtually guaranteed to end in victory. So hang in there. You'll be very glad you did.

Reward Yourself

There are many ways to be a hero in life, and not all of them involve saving people from floods or burning buildings. Sometimes being a hero means quietly putting your ego and fears aside and doing what it takes to protect your future and that of your loved ones.

That's what you're doing each time you make your ten calls. It's both hard and heroic, and you deserve the occasional reward—whether it's dinner at your favorite restaurant or a visit to the massage therapist. So every time you reach a milestone, whether it's making your first contact with a hiring manager or successfully presenting yourself and getting invited to an interview, say "thanks" to yourself by treating yourself to something you enjoy. You've earned it.

Scored Your First Interview? Congratulations— Now Keep Moving Forward!

The first interview you earn by direct-calling a hiring manager will be one of the sweetest moments of your life. However, if that success comes before the final day of your fifteen-day campaign, keep making your calls. Getting one interview is outstanding, but it's even better to get two, three, or even more. Each interview you get puts you in a better bargaining position, and there's a good chance that the second or third firm that invites you for an interview will make a far better offer than the first.

Moreover, in today's business climate, an interview is no guarantee of a job. Companies often interview dozens of candidates for each job, so there are no sure bets and it's smart to line up as many opportunities as you can.

When you follow your campaign through to its conclusion, you'll often get a bonus in the form of additional calls that come in well after you've finished your campaign. These contacts could be extremely valuable, either during this job hunt or in the future. So no matter how many interviews you line up, stick to your goals and additional rewards will follow. In today's volatile job market, you can't have too many good contacts.

When you complete your fifteen-day action plan and land your interviews, you'll be a giant step closer to getting a new or better job. But getting those crucial interviews, while it's the hardest step, isn't the final one. Even when you get a foot in the door, you'll still be competing with a host of people who are just as hungry for a new opportunity as you are. The next chapter will show you how to maximize the chances that when you go for that hard-earned interview, you'll be the candidate who gets the offer.

PART THREE

Following Through:
How to Nail the Job

CHAPTER SIX

The Phone Interview

As your calls result in success, you'll move into Phase Two of your job hunt: the telephone interview. It's great when a contact with a job opportunity calls back, but you need to learn how to parlay that phone conversation into a face-to-face meeting. This chapter will outline the homework you need to do before the call, the techniques you can use to establish a rapport with the caller, and why it's important to recognize that you still have to win the interviewer over during this stage.

You've scored your first hit: one of your direct-calling contacts wants to return the favor by calling you for a phone interview. If you can pass this initial screening, you're a big step closer to landing a job—but don't expect it to be a slam-dunk.

Back when jobs went begging, companies often dismissed phone interviews as a formality, if they conducted them at all. If you had the right qualifications, and didn't make a fool of yourself during a brief conversation, you almost always got invited to a face-to-face interview. Now, however, employers in many fields have a large pool of candidates, and they can be far more selective. As a result, it's no longer safe to think of the telephone interview as a "gimme," even if you're highly qualified for the job that's being offered. These days, firms tend to screen more candidates for each job, and screen them more intensively, than in earlier years.

Moreover, the very fact that you're having a phone interview means that you need to be on your toes. Why? *Because if you'd already won the heart of your potential employer, they would skip this stage and invite you directly to a face-to-face interview.* If you're scheduled for a phone interview, they like you . . . but they don't love you yet.

To make them love you, and advance yourself to the next stage, you'll need to impress your telephone interviewer with most or all of these:

- Your communication skills

- Your talent for mastering new skills

- Your creativity

- Your grasp of the "big picture"

- Your ability to deal with complex issues and problems

- Your experience and its relevance to your potential employer's needs

- Your skill at reading interpersonal situations and responding in the right way

- Your ability to be either a "self-starter" or a team player, depending on the needs of the firm that's interviewing you

- Your ability to focus on either a specific project or a long-term commitment

- Your willingness to accept a compensation package that's commensurate with what the company can offer

In short, the company's goal at this stage is to determine if you're a good fit for them. Will your personality mesh with their culture? Do your skills and experience fit their needs? Will you complement the existing team? Will your expectations when it comes to salary and other compensation be in line with theirs?

--- **T**ALE from the **TRENCHES** ---

A recruiter was conducting a phone screening with a candidate vying for a senior-level technical position at a semiconductor company. The candidate expected lots of questions about his technical expertise, but instead, the company asked the recruiter to hone in on how well he'd fit into their corporate culture. Rather than delving deeply into the candidate's experience with SOC integrated circuit design, the recruiter asked questions such as, "How did you interact with your peers in your last position?" and "Do you do well in a competitive environment?" Other candidates received the exact same questions, and many of them fumbled for answers. But fortunately this candidate had researched the company's philosophy and style as well as its products. Because he'd prepared so diligently, he had no difficulty acing the phone interview and was promptly scheduled for an onsite meeting.

Demonstrating that you're a perfect match in so many areas, all in the course of a short phone call with a complete stranger, is a tall order—especially since eight out of ten phone or face-to-face interviews are won or lost during the first five minutes of the conversation. To make matters more complicated, you'll have no clue ahead of time as to which elements of "good fit" your interviewer will want to explore.

The moral is that you can never overprepare for an interview, whether it's on the phone or in person. It's easy to become complacent, especially if you've done a few phone interviews that went well, and think, "I've got this down pat." Each call will be different from your last one, however, and that means that each call requires the same intense level of preparation. Maximize your chances of success by doing your homework up front.

Nail Down Your References

Now is the time to call former managers and colleagues and ask if you can use them as references, if you haven't already done so. You probably won't want to give out your references' names during the early stages of interviewing—more on that later in this chapter—but you'll need to be prepared in case a company moves quickly in the hiring process.

It's best to contact four former managers and three former coworkers. If you're just starting out and don't have that many business contacts, call your college professors or individuals at organizations where you've done volunteer work.

Give these people plenty of lead-time, so they can come up with positive and well-thought-out comments. Also, remind them about your major accomplishments (especially those related to the job you're seeking), so they can highlight these achievements if they're called.

Set the Stage for Your Call

Make sure you're ready, both mentally and physically, for a phone interview. Begin by reviewing all of the facts you've compiled about the firm that will be contacting you. If there's time, do a quick search to uncover any new data or recent news. Also, review the reasons why you're an excellent choice for the firm's opening. Make notes about the company's projects and goals, and how your skills and experience mesh with the company's needs.

Phone Manners: What Messages Do You Send?

How you handle a phone call is as important as what you say. Some candidates' voices transmit the message that they're discouraged, or even rude. Conversely, other candidates make an outstanding impression simply by using common courtesy. They thank the interviewer for calling, speak in an upbeat tone, pause to carefully consider questions before answering, and tactfully handle any interruptions by children or neighbors. At a time when nearly every job attracts more than one qualified candidate, decisions often come down to an interviewer's intuition. It's critical that your caller thinks, "What a nice/confident/poised individual," rather than, "Ugh." Also, if you're asked to place a call to an interviewer at a specific time, make sure you're on time or a minute or two early. If you don't get through, leave a message on voice mail or with an assistant—and if you have your contact's e-mail address, send a quick note explaining that you tried to call. That way, your contact won't mistakenly think that he or she was "stood up."

Next, make sure you have all of your essential tools by the phone. These include your Company Research Worksheet and Hiring Contact Status Report form (see Chapter Four), your resume, a notepad and pen, a calendar, and a glass or bottle of water in case your throat gets dry during a long call.

If you live with other people, make sure they understand that you'll need their help in making your call go well. It's not always possible to control a barking dog or crying baby, but arrange ahead of time to minimize distractions. Let children know that they need to leave the room when a call comes in, and ask family members to handle any other noise problems.

If there's too much commotion when a call comes in, it's fine to say, "Thank you for calling—would you mind holding on for just a moment? " That will buy time for you to turn off the TV, chase out the kids or the dog, and clear your head so you can give your full attention to your caller. If an unexpected caller asks to conduct a phone interview on the spot, and the timing is totally wrong for you, ask for the caller's phone number and schedule a mutually convenient time to call back. However, say "yes" to an immediate interview if you know you're prepared. They may be testing your responsiveness and flexibility in dealing with unexpected situations.

Focus on the Caller's Needs

A typical phone interview lasts thirty to forty-five minutes; you'll probably talk with a hiring manager, human resources staff person, or corporate recruiter. Your caller could also be a team or group leader, or the hiring manager's boss. Sometimes you'll arrange an interview with one person and then wind up talking with someone different, so be prepared for any contingency.

In most cases, after a brief introduction and opening comments, a telephone interviewer will start by asking you about yourself: "Why are you interested in our company?" "What are your career goals?" "What are your strengths?" It's tempting to fall in with this conversational flow, but the most important thing to remember during phone interviews is to do what *doesn't* come naturally: turn the tables, and talk about the company instead.

Job seekers enjoy talking about their own interests and experiences, but you'll enhance your chances if you discreetly redirect the conversation from you ("here's what I like/dislike/want to do") to them ("what are your goals/what makes your product unique/what do you expect of the person doing this job?") When you employ this strategy, you'll impress your caller and gain knowledge you can use to sell yourself as a perfect fit for the company's needs.

The trick to turning a "me" conversation into a "you" conversation lies in your timing. There are a thousand and one ways a phone interview can go, so you need to stay alert for openings that will allow you steer the conversation back to the needs of the company and how you can meet them. Here's an example:

> INTERVIEWER: "Why are you interested in our company?"
>
> CANDIDATE: "In researching your company, I've learned that you are one of the best in the business in system-on-chip designs for microprocessors. I understand that you have a new project underway, and I have experience in the exact technology you are using. Are you using RTL design in your next SOC design?"

Here's another example, using a different question:

> INTERVIEWER: "What do you like most about working in customer support?"

CANDIDATE: "I really enjoy working one-on-one with customers. My current manager always directs difficult callers my way because I know how to deal with them effectively. I understand that your firm's marketing emphasizes the high ratings you receive for customer service in comparison with your competitors in the insurance industry. Also, I recently read that your company was designated as number 1 in customer satisfaction by *Consumer Reports*. Based on that, I'm guessing that you have a need for experienced people who know how to deal with customers tactfully and efficiently."

Note that in both of these examples, the candidate goes a step beyond the question that's being asked. It would be easy to respond, in each case, by saying, "I'm interested in your company because I think it's a good place to work." Instead of giving a typical but unimaginative answer, both of our fictional candidates used this opportunity to

- Show their knowledge of the companies' products or services

- Show how their skills dovetail with the companies' goals

The first candidate goes further, by ending with a smart question that will lead the interviewer to offer more clues about the company's needs. This is a powerful strategy, and one you should employ yourself. Seek out opportunities during your interview to ask intelligent questions based on what you learned about the company during your research. (For instance, "I understand that you're working on a new intrusion-detection software program. How does it compare to the systems that ISS and Axent offer?")

As you talk, continue to focus on how your skills can contribute to your caller's current goals For example: "Given your center's interest in expanding your preschool activities to include athletics, I'm thinking my previous experience with the Parks and Recreation Department's athletic programs could be a major asset." If possible, cite specifics about how you can contribute to the firm's goals. For example, "I read that you're working on improving the accuracy of your fill-and-seal machines. I worked on a similar product upgrade several years ago, and our results exceeded the client's specifications." In short, at every opportunity, think "them" instead of "you," and answer accordingly.

Prepare for the "What Would You Do?" Question

One method that's popular with today's interviewers is called *behavioral interviewing*. Interviewers who use this approach will typically ask you for a situation-behavior-outcome example—in other words, "name a problem you encountered, explain what you did to solve it, and tell me what happened as a result." Here's a quick example of a good response:

> "One firm that contracted with me needed to hire sixty employees in a ninety-day period. I defined the position requirements with the VP of my client group, determined which hires had priority, mapped out the appropriate sequencing and timing of hires, and built a plan to identify highly qualified candidates using a variety of sources. I implemented this plan, and, as I located candidates, I structured interview teams, coordinated phone and onsite interviews, and offered an orientation process for candidates selected for hiring. As a result of this coordinated effort, the project was completed on time and under budget, saving the company $260,000 by eliminating the need for costly search-firm and agency hires."

The behavioral interview question comes in a variety of flavors, and you can't predict which version your interviewer will prefer. The best way to prepare for any approach is to write down specific responses to a variety of scenarios, so you'll be ready with an answer instead of hesitating or stammering. Below are typical variations on behavioral interview questions. You should jot down some answers you can cite in response:

- Give an example of a time when you had to "go the extra mile" in order to get a job done.

- Tell me about a time when you used persuasion/presentation skills/logic to solve a problem.

- Tell me about a time you dealt with a problem colleague/boss/client/customer.

- Tell me about the most difficult decision you ever made in your career.

- Tell me about a time when you anticipated potential problems and prevented them.

- Tell me about a time when you successfully dealt with a stressful situation/a tight deadline/an unpleasant situation.

Some interviewers flip the behavioral question around, asking about a negative experience—e.g., "Tell me about a time you failed at a task," or "Describe a situation in which you left a customer dissatisfied." If you're asked such a question, this is not the time for an in-depth, soul-searching discussion of your weaknesses. Instead, try to think of a situation in which you come away a problem solver—e.g.,

"We had one angry customer at the bank that my staff and I simply couldn't satisfy. I learned later, from another employee, that this customer had experienced a serious problem several years earlier when the bank made a major error in her account, and she was hostile because she continued to expect bad service. Once I understood the situation, I made it a point to 'go the extra mile' for her each time she came in. In addition, I explained the situation to my coworkers, and asked them to do the same thing. It took time, but eventually she became one of our most satisfied customers."

Or, if you're asked a question such as, "Name a big mistake you've made," give an example but follow it up in a positive way; for example, "When I first started working in sales, I made an error while making a customer refund. It was embarrassing, but I learned a great deal from the mistake. In fact, I'm now the person my current company turns to when it's time to train new employees about dealing with customer refunds." Whenever you can, turn a negative question into a positive response.

Sometimes you simply won't be able to conjure up a reply to a behavioral question. At these times, just say, "I don't believe I've encountered that situation before." Always be honest about what you have and haven't done.

Good Answers for Other Routine Questions

Every interviewer has his or her playbook, but some questions crop up over and over again. Several of these questions are so basic—for instance, "Tell me about your current responsibilities"—that the responses will be obvious. Others, however, are tougher to answer unless you're well prepared. Some of these challenging questions follow.

"What type of position are you looking for?"

As you answer this question, remember that both you and the interviewer are looking for "fit"—how good a match you are for the company, and vice versa. If possible, give an open-ended response, rather than a specific one that might fail to match your caller's expectations. For instance, rather than saying, "I'm seeking a position as a senior housekeeping supervisor," say, "I'm looking for an opportunity to use the experience I've gained in supervising large staffs at three different four-star hotels. I'm not as concerned about my title as I am about my responsibilities and how I can contribute."

"Why are you looking for a position?"

If you're currently employed, you're sure to be asked some variant of this question, and the right answer will score you points. You want to have a response that is similar to: "I'd like the opportunity to work in an environment that offers greater challenges, and rewards hard work and results." Keep your answer focused on the positive aspects of your move, rather than on any negative aspects of your current situation.

If you're not currently employed because you lost your job in a mass layoff, your project was cancelled, or your employer went out of business, answering this question is equally simple. Explain what happened, and talk about the efforts you're making to find a new position. Your description of the work you're putting into researching and targeting companies requiring your skills will impress your caller.

But what if you and your last employer didn't hit it off, and you quit or got fired as a result? Or what if you're hoping to leave a dead-end job that you hate? In either of these situations, you'll want to be careful how you reply. If you're in this position, the most important rule to remember is: *Don't bad-mouth your previous or current boss, no matter what.* Instead, say that your skills didn't mesh with the company's new direction, or come up with an equally positive reply. It's a huge mistake to trash your old supervisors or coworkers, even if they deserve it, because it makes you sound like a whiner or a problem employee. If you're switching jobs because you hated your boss, hit a "glass ceiling" at your previous workplace, found the work boring, or didn't make enough money, simply be honest and answer that you're looking to grow your career and take your professional development to the next level.

"Tell me about the gaps in your resume."

Here again, honesty is the best policy. There's no shame in an employment gap; the only shame is if you try to cover it up or lie about it. Employers realize that plenty of outstanding workers experience periods of joblessness. If there's a different explanation for a hole in your resume—for instance, if you went back to school or took a six-month break between jobs in order to care for a parent with Alzheimer's—simply explain this. Honesty is appreciated, while dishonesty—if it's detected—won't be tolerated.

"What are your strengths?"

Be ready with a list of at least five or six areas in which you shine. These could range from "I'm willing to work long hours" to "I'm self-motivated" to "I'm a good team player." Other qualities to mention include loyalty, integrity, promptness, good communication skills, and the ability to learn new skills quickly. Most importantly, be ready to cite some specific work examples to back up your claims.

"What are your weaknesses?"

Again, this is not a time for baring your soul. Keep your major flaws to yourself, and instead pick something minor. For instance, you could say that you hate filing—as long as filing skills aren't the least bit important for the position you're seeking.

"Tell me about yourself."

This question typically is asked only by inexperienced or unskilled interviewers. However, you should be ready to offer a unique response, so you'll stand out from your competitors. Most people respond by listing their skills or experience, facts that the caller probably already knows from your resume. Demonstrate that you're different, by focusing on an intangible—"I have a reputation for delivering quality results, especially under pressure." Or leave the caller with a memorable detail such as, "I love to set and meet tough goals, both in my personal life and in my business life. For instance, I've climbed four of the world's ten tallest mountains. I bring that same intensity to getting results for my employers."

As you're talking, refer frequently to your Company Research Worksheet, where you listed the reason why you're a good fit for your caller's jobs. Make sure you cover each point on your list. It's easy to get flustered or off track during a conversation, and keeping your notes at hand will ensure that you work all of your strongest points into the conversation.

Limit Yourself to "Deal-Breaker" Questions

Some job sites recommend asking a whole laundry list of questions at the telephone interview stage—e.g., "What is your working environment like?" "What are the opportunities for advancement?" "Do you offer employee training?" "How much autonomy would I have?"

This is not the best approach at this stage, because the face-to-face interview is a better place for delving into a firm's strong and weak points. Besides, if you've done your homework by visiting the company's Web site, and checking Vault.com, Hoover's, and similar sites (see Chapter Four), you probably already have a good picture of the firm's culture, benefits, and management style.

However, do make sure you clarify any basic and critical details before you hang up. These may include: Does the job truly involve your particular skill set? If it's a consulting job, is it strictly consulting or is it a consult-to-hire position? If the job is in sales, is it salaried or straight commission? Is extensive travel required? If you are disabled, is the company's worksite accessible? As a general rule, ask "what's in it for me?" questions at this stage only if the answers are critical.

Don't Dance Around the Salary Issue

People often advise you to be coy if you're asked about your expected salary. However, at the end of the day, your decision whether to accept a position, or even to invest more time pursuing it, will come down to hard numbers. If your needs can't be met by what your caller is willing to offer, why waste everyone's time? Skip the games, and give your caller a straight answer about the base salary you expect, as well as any bonuses or noncash compensation. The caller will let you know if your numbers are too high, and will respect you for your honesty—and you won't expend unnecessary effort competing for a job that turns out to pay $10,000 less than the bare minimum you can afford to live on.

If you've been working at the same job for years, it's time to get a reality check on what current salaries are for your field. In some technical or manufacturing fields, salaries are significantly lower than they were in a few years ago. In other fields, such as nursing, salaries are rising. So before you say "yes" or "no" to a salary offer, talk with recruiters or colleagues in your field and find out what your current market value is (see Chapter Eight for more on this).

Think Twice Before Offering Your References

There's a chance that your interviewer will ask you if you're willing to provide references at this stage. If that happens, be happy that matters are progressing so rapidly, but also be cautious. Sadly, some hiring managers may have an ulterior motive in asking for references early in the interviewing game. An unscrupulous manager may call your contact references and recruit them directly, perhaps even for the job that you're trying to get.

If you feel very comfortable with the caller and the circumstances, go ahead and supply references as early as the phone interview stage. But if you have any doubts, simply say that you'd prefer to wait—or, if you don't want to risk offending the caller, respond that you need to get in touch with your references to make sure you have permission to use their names.

Move to the Next Stage

If you're convinced by the end of the phone interview that the job is right for you, convey your interest to your caller, and ask about the next step in the interviewing process. Also inquire about the hiring timetable, so you'll know what to expect.

Your caller is likely to respond by inviting you to a face-to-face interview. Find out, either during the call or afterward, the names of the interviewers and their positions in the company; the date and time of the interview; and what information, if any, you'll be expected to bring. Also, verify that you have your caller's name (correctly spelled), e-mail address, and telephone number.

If your interviewer doesn't offer an invitation to a face-to-face interview, ask if he or she has any areas of concern. Try to clear up any misunderstandings, and then ask again about the next step and timetable. You can also ask, "May I give you a call to follow up if I haven't heard from you by next Friday?" Be sure, at the end of the call, to thank the interviewer once again for considering you for a position.

If you've done your homework, you're likely to advance to the next stage in the interview process. However, if you get a cool response, that's probably a signal that you haven't won over your caller. Don't allow this to depress or discourage you, because virtually every job hunter gets a few "no's" at the phone interview stage. Job-hunting is a numbers game, and each interview, successful or not, brings you one step closer to getting the work you're seeking. Learn what you can from each experience, and then move on.

Do be sure to make a record of how your call went, using your Hiring Contact Status Report. Take several minutes to analyze what went well and what didn't, so you can make an even stronger presentation in the future.

Send a Note

It's smart to send a thank-you note after each stage of the interview process. This can be a quick e-mail or a jotted note sent by mail. Say that you appreciated the interviewer's time and that you hope that you will be able to work together.

You can also use this note to express your enthusiasm for the job and to remind the contact about your strengths ("I'm pleased that my office management skills are such a good match for your needs."). In addition, you can quickly clear up any possible misunderstandings, or bring up points you forgot to mention on the phone. Most candidates neglect to send thank-you notes, so your extra effort will help you to stand out from the crowd.

Watch Your "e-Etiquette"

Often you'll need to e-mail a contact before or after a phone or face-to-face interview to clarify an appointment time, send additional data, or gently probe for information if you haven't heard back after an interview. When it's time to send a message, don't underestimate the importance of writing it right. You'd be surprised how easy it is to lose a job opportunity in the time it takes to send an e-mail. Conversely, you can use even a brief e-mail message to show a prospective employer that you're intelligent, considerate, and efficient.

To make sure that your e-mail sends the right message, follow these simple rules.

Rule #1: Use a businesslike e-mail address

This point was mentioned earlier in reference to resumes, but it bears repeating here. If you can afford it, use something more sophisticated than an AOL or Hotmail address. But no matter what service you use, pick an e-mail address that sounds professional. Some variation of your name is best (e.g., *bgraham@briangrahamco.com*, or *brian.graham@briangrahamco.com*).

Rule #2: Respond promptly to requests for additional information

This is especially crucial if an employer requests information that can make or break your chances—for instance, proof of a certification or security clearance. But it's important even if a request is minor, because a timely reply will tell the person at the other end that you're efficient and follow through on tasks.

If you can't respond immediately to a request, let the person at the other end know why (e.g., "I'm leaving for the airport in two minutes for a quick trip to San Francisco, but I will fax the information you requested as quickly as possible upon my return Thursday morning.").

Rule #3: Proofread each e-mail at least twice before you send it

An occasional typo is fine when you're communicating with friends or relatives, but mistakes can be fatal when you're writing to a potential boss or interviewer. If writing is a weak point for you, don't rely on your spell checker. Instead, see if you can arrange to run your e-mails by a grammar-and-spelling savvy friend for a quick proofing before sending them.

Rule #4: Don't be too casual

Avoid being stuffy, but don't be too informal or "cutesy" either. Let the person who's e-mailing you set the tone, and follow it. It's fine to use the other person's first name if the contact has already established that you're on a first-name basis; otherwise, stick to Mr. or Ms.

Rule # 5: Keep it short and to the point

You're corresponding with busy people, and they don't have time for long-winded e-mails. Unless there's a good reason for running longer, keep your e-mails down to two short paragraphs.

Rule #6: Don't type in caps

An all-caps word in an e-mail is generally interpreted as "yelling" and looks unprofessional, so avoid sending a message like, "I'm REALLY looking forward to meeting you."

Rule #7: Assertive doesn't mean aggressive

Many firms keep job hunters dangling for weeks, and a few never get back to interviewees at all. This is incredibly rude, but needless to say, it won't do you any good to express your irritation to your contact. Instead, send a friendly note like this:

> Dear Jane,
>
> I'm just checking in to see if you might need any additional information from me. I enjoyed meeting you and Paul, and appreciated the opportunity to interview for the position as your administrative assistant. If you have any information you're able to share about how the interview process is moving along, I'd very much appreciate hearing from you. Thank you!
>
> Sincerely . . .

Generally a note like this will elicit some type of reply, without making you appear to be leaning on the recipient.

CHAPTER SEVEN

The Face-to-Face Interview

To succeed at a job interview, you need to understand the needs and goals of your target company and retool your interview techniques and your expectations in response. This chapter covers what to know about the company and its key personnel ahead of time, the best way to handle both standard and trick questions, and the correct way to follow up after an interview.

Congratulations—you've scored an in-person interview at one of your target companies. Now it's time for you to nail down a job offer, by doing everything right. When you reach the face-to-face interview stage you're more than halfway home, because most of your rivals are out of the picture. On the other hand, your remaining competition is likely to be fierce, and your chances of being selected could hinge on a few crucial questions. That's why, to maximize your chances of success, you'll need to shine on the day of your interview—and to do that, you'll need to start preparing now. Here's how.

Review Your Research

Nearly all of the questions you'll be asked at your face-to-face interview will be predictable, and many will be repeats from your phone interview. However, it's still crucial to do your homework before your interview date. Being underprepared can lose you a job, but being overprepared never will!

Get a notepad and pen, and pull out the notes you took during your phone interview, as well as all of the data you've accumulated on your potential employer. As you read though this material, list all of the critical facts you've uncovered about the firm and its people, and determine exactly how you can sell yourself to them. You did this earlier—once before you started making your direct calls, and again before your telephone interview. This time, however, you'll be building an even more powerful case for yourself by incorporating the new knowledge you picked up from your phone contact. Ask yourself: "Which of my skills most impressed the caller?" and "What aspects of my experience did the caller zero in on?" Refine your interview approach accordingly.

In addition, if you've been given the names of your interview team, take a few minutes to research them on the Internet. This can provide you with facts about their professional or personal interests that will help you to establish a rapport and avoid conversational missteps.

As you make your notes, refer to the list of questions below. This is known as the "interviewer scorecard." Almost all managers use an assessment similar to this to rate potential candidates; thus, it's smart to tailor your responses accordingly ahead of time.

Primary Responsibilities—Do you have the skills and experience needed to perform the core tasks of the job?

Supporting and Secondary Responsibilities—Are you qualified to undertake additional duties associated with this job?

Management and Organizational Skills—Do you have what it takes to supervise other employees or to keep a complicated project on target?

Opportunities for Improvement—Are you smart, flexible, and willing to take on new tasks and master new skills?

Complex Tasks—Can you handle a many-faceted project and see it through successfully from beginning to end?

Technical Abilities—Are your tech skills relevant and up-to-date?

Team and People Skills—How well do you deal with supervisors, coworkers, or customers?

Projects and Deliverables—What specific projects or outcomes can you offer as proof that you're the right person for this job?

Additional Skills and Experience—What special ability or expertise sets you apart from other candidates?

Briefly outline your strengths in each of these categories, listing specific examples to support your statements. For example: "Highly capable at planning and carrying out complex tasks—cite successful planning and implementation of a charity ball that raised $50,000." When you're done, use your notes to create loose scripts for answering the questions you're most likely to encounter. We talked earlier about the importance of rehearsing your direct calls, just as an actor rehearses for a role. It's equally important to practice your lines before a face-to-face interview. Your goal isn't to memorize answers, but rather to make sure you have your selling points firmly in mind. When you're finished with your research and your rehearsal, place your notes with your other interview materials, so you can refer to them during your interview.

Review Your Resume

If your resume is an extensive document, take a minute to review it. Few things are more embarrassing than being asked about some long-ago or seemingly minor event listed on your resume—for instance, a brief stint writing SQL code before you became a network administrator—and saying, "Uh . . . I'm not sure I remember that." Such lapses occur more often than you'd think, especially to people with long work records or to consultants who do lots of short-term projects. Avoid this mistake by making sure you're familiar with every detail on the version of your resume that your interviewers received.

Get Your Facts Together

Most interviewers ask for a work and salary history, so prepare a list of the dates of your last five jobs, your previous managers' names and titles, and your compensation for these jobs. If you've received an application form, fill it out now. Also, sign any drug screening or background check forms you received. If you didn't receive any forms ahead of time, consider calling the HR department and asking them to send any required forms to you. This can save lots of time on your interview day.

Be sure to get the names and job titles of the people who will be interviewing you. Ask for the spellings of their names, and, if you're afraid you might forget how to pronounce them, make a quick note (e.g., "Bob Deighlough as in Day-Low") so you'll remember. Be sure to get a contact number, so you can call if problems arise.

Beware of the "Trapdoor" Interview

Most companies will happily provide you with the names of your interview team, but some will say, "We're not sure who'll be talking with you." This is a red flag, because it usually means one thing: The company wants an easy out if you don't immediately measure up to their expectations. Be prepared if you're scheduled for a "no-name" interview, because there's a chance that your interviewer will decide within minutes that you're not right for the job—without ever giving you a chance to prove otherwise—and give you a quick brush-off. If this happens, learn what you can from the experience and move on.

If possible, find out if you are going to be interviewed by several people in a group meeting, or undergo a series of one-on-one interviews. Also find out if any type of testing will be involved.

Last but not least, make sure your cell phone is charged—and if you don't have one, buy or borrow one. Complications such as a flat tire or a traffic jam can throw you off schedule on an interview day, and if that happens, rapid communication is imperative. If you carry a cell phone, you'll be able to handle crises in an efficient way and notify your interviewers so they won't be stewing when you arrive.

Plan a Visual Display of Your Skills

No matter what career field you're in, or how much experience you have, it's an excellent idea to incorporate a "show and tell" into your job interview. The cliché about a picture being worth a thousand words is true, because people remember 80 percent of what they see, and only 20 percent of what they hear. When you offer visible evidence of your accomplishments, your interviewer will be highly impressed, not just by your skills but also by your initiative in being prepared. The samples you prepare should be as closely related to the company's products or services as possible. Among the types of items you can assemble are:

- Diagrams or outlines of projects.

- Work samples. For example, if you're a graphic designer, bring brochures or artwork you've designed.

- Examples of major projects you completed as a student, if you are new to the job market. These could include a master's thesis on a topic related to the firm's work, the blueprints for a gadget that won a national design award, or any other hard evidence of skills related to the job you're seeking.

- Favorable news items about your work: a newspaper article lauding a successful public relations event you organized, for instance, or a business journal's rave review about a product whose development you spearheaded.

- Letters of commendation. One young programmer fresh out of the Navy brought a copy of a letter from an Admiral commending him for making a software change that resulted in fleet-wide efficiency improvements. As a result, he was selected over several far more experienced candidates.

Plan to bring several copies of your exhibit to the interview, in binders or manila folders. You'll want to have them readily at hand so you can wait for the right moment to interject, "I'm glad you mentioned that . . . let me show you what I've brought that speaks to that point," and pull out your material.

This small effort can make a huge difference in the selection process. Employers assume that candidates who go to the trouble of providing work samples at an interview will also take extra pains to achieve in the workplace—and in almost every case, they're right.

How to Ace Your Interview Day

Plan on arriving ten to fifteen minutes early for your interview. Getting there too early will make you look anxious, and arriving too late will make you look rude. When you get to the interview site, be respectful of everyone you meet, from parking lot guards to receptionists. Also, turn off your cell phone or pager, so it won't disturb your interviewers during your meeting.

As you greet your interviewers, be conscious of your nonverbal communication. It's normal to be a little nervous, and your interviewers will understand that; however, it's important to project confidence and enthusiasm. During the interview, avoid assuming a "defensive" posture—shrinking into your chair, or crossing your arms across your chest—or looking jittery (tapping toes, fiddling fingers). Instead, adopt an "open" posture, by leaning forward a little, making eye contact with your interviewers, and smiling naturally.

If you're interviewing with several people at once, make a point of acknowledging each of them, even if only one of them is asking most of the questions. It's polite, and it'll increase your rapport with each participant. Also, give each questioner's inquiries equal attention and consideration, even if some questions are more on the mark than others. And answer every question straightforwardly, because even a small white lie during an interview can cause you grief later on.

As with the phone interview, take time to consider each question carefully, and answer thoughtfully. (See Chapter Six for additional advice on handling specific interview questions.) If you need more time to formulate an answer, ask your interviewer to repeat the question. Above all, remember the cardinal rule: *Keep bringing the conversation back to the company's goals and how you can contribute to them.* At every opportunity, give concrete examples of how your skills mesh with your interviewer's needs.

Make sure you introduce your work sample—preferably early on in the interview. If an opportunity for "show and tell" doesn't arise naturally, wait until you're well into the interview and subtly steer the topic in a direction that will allow you to present your materials.

Handling Hostility or Trick Questions

One unpleasant situation you might encounter is an interview in which an employer seeks to intimidate you by constantly interrupting you, disagreeing with you, or otherwise putting you on the spot. Your best defense in this situation is simply to play along. Your secret weapon is the knowledge that this antagonism is a game, and that your tormenter simply wants to see if you can maintain your composure. If you stay polite, calm, and even-tempered no matter how rudely the interviewer behaves, you'll demonstrate confidence and maturity.

One good thing about a stress interview is it offers you an important clue about how the company operates, and gives you fair warning to think twice about accepting a job. If a key employee truly believes that rudeness is an excellent strategy for dealing with a complete stranger, imagine what it would be like to work with that same person every day—and then ask yourself what kind of company would put him or her in a position of power.

Handling Improper Questions

If your interviewer says something that makes you uncomfortable, you should tactfully steer the conversation back to a more suitable topic. But what if the question is outright illegal? Many hiring managers aren't experts on the law, and they may innocently ask questions that are inappropriate. This includes any questions about your marital status, religion, age, whether you're planning to have children, the status of a military discharge, national origin or citizenship, whether you've ever been arrested, or if you have a disability or medical condition (although an employer *is* allowed to ask if you are physically capable of performing a particular task). If you're asked an illegal question, use your judgment. The interviewer could simply be making friendly small talk. If that's the case, it's smart to answer politely. Of course, you're well within your rights to say, "You can't ask me that question—it's illegal." It is good common sense to be kind and courteous, but it's also fine to tactfully draw the line on suspect questions that do not have job relevance.

A less repugnant but still annoying interview technique is the trick question, much prized by Microsoft and occasionally used by other companies. Truly good recruiters and hiring managers don't place a lot of stock in employing trick questions to select a candidate. Such techniques might show that a candidate is creative, but they might also simply reveal that the candidate found the answer on the Internet or in a book. Moreover, a candidate who can't think of an answer might simply be very nervous; even the most gifted person can have trouble thinking creatively in the artificial atmosphere of an interview. More importantly, the ability to answer a brainteaser tells little or nothing about how a candidate will respond to real-life situations.

If you're asked a trick question and can't think of an answer, simply tell the truth: Say that you're drawing a blank, and then steer the interview back to your qualifications. Don't worry too much about how this answer affects your chances, because if an interviewer rules you out for a job solely because you couldn't invent a pat reply to "How would you sell ice to an Eskimo?" or "How many gas stations are there in the United States?" you're probably better off somewhere else.

The tempo of your interview will depend largely on the personalities of the interview team and the number of people involved. Let your interviewers set the pace, and follow their lead. If they seem to be hurrying you along and you can tell that they're in a rush to get back to other obligations, do your best to answer questions quickly and concisely, and keep chitchat to a minimum. If they're relaxed and talkative, follow their leisurely pace and be careful not to rush your answers. By being responsive to your interviewers' cues, you'll help to convince them that you're a good fit for their team.

Assess the Corporate Culture

As you're talking, keep your eyes open for clues about the company's "culture"—that is, the attitudes, beliefs, and ethical values that shape a company's behavior toward its employees and customers. Does the company value its people? Does it treat them fairly, or take advantage of them? Do people enjoy working there? What does the company consider acceptable behavior, both *by* and *toward* its employees?

If you're new to the job market, it's easy to underestimate how important corporate culture can be. But it's no exaggeration to say that the "personality" of your firm can dramatically affect your productivity, your happiness, and the quality of your life—both on and off the job. A company's culture will determine everything from how much overtime your bosses will demand and how much decision-making authority you'll have, to whether you can wear music headphones at work, decorate your desk with family photos, or leave early for your child's school play.

Needless to say, if a company's corporate culture leaves something to be desired, your interviewers will try to hide that problem from you. Conversely, interviewers at companies with good corporate cultures may not think to point out their advantages. Thus, it's vital to form your own opinions, based on what you see. You'll pick up many hints about your target firm's corporate culture by watching how your interviewers act. Other evidence will be obvious if you look and listen. Among the signs to watch for:

1. Do your interviewers seem comfortable and open, or do they defer timidly to the most senior interviewer and seem cautious (or even nervous) about expressing their own opinions?

2. Do your interviewers freely make positive comments about the company—and, if so, do they seem sincere?

3. Conversely, do they sometimes make negative comments about the company? If so, are they made in a teasing way (which most likely indicates a free environment where humor is allowed), or do you sense an undercurrent of frustration or even hostility toward the firm?

4. Do the people you've seen so far, including both the inter- view team and other people you saw in passing, seem happy and enthusiastic, or stressed and depressed?

5. Is the environment casual or businesslike? Highly structured or flexible? Friendly or buttoned-down?

6. Does chronic overtime appear to be the norm?

7. Does the company appear to operate in an organized and understandable way, and do employees have clearly defined roles and goals?

Also, pay attention to your physical surroundings. If you're able to get a look at the computers or other pieces of equipment, notice whether they're modern and adequate for the company's work, or shoddy and out-of-date. Evaluate whether the work areas are attractive and welcoming or sterile and impersonal. And notice the presence or lack of amenities such as convenient parking, a well-stocked lunchroom, and clean and adequate restrooms. Often, the look of a company's physical plant is a reflection of how well it treats its employees.

A company's culture is more critical than *any other factor* in determining how you'll do in your new position. A rewarding cul- ture will challenge, encourage, and reward you. In a toxic culture, you'll be mistreated, ignored, or stressed and, before you know it, you'll be looking for another job. So stay alert for the clues that will tell you whether your potential employer's culture is healthy or toxic, and ask yourself, "Does this look like an environment where I can thrive?"

Look for "Buy" Signals

During the opening stages of an interview, you'll be busy fielding questions initiated by the interview team. As your meeting progresses, however, watch for signals that indicate that your listeners are growing more interested and positive. These can include positive body language, comments that show the interviewers are impressed by your skills, or a shift toward questions about what your requirements for taking the job would be. When you spot this positive feedback—or when your interviewer turns to you and asks, "Is there anything you'd like to know about us?"—it's time to begin asking questions of your own.

What questions should you ask? Forget the ones that many job candidates ask at the interview stage such as "What kind of health plan do you have?" "How many vacation days would I get?" You'll learn all of these details later, when you receive an offer, and you can evaluate the merits of the company's benefits and perks at that point. Posing these questions now, however, can weaken your chances, rather than strengthening them, by making it appear that you're more interested in your own concerns than in the company's needs.

Instead, ask strategic, high-level questions that will accomplish the following goals:

- Reinforce your "rightness" for the position.

- Steer your interviewers into answering your questions as though you were already on the job, and thus encourage them to visualize your hiring as a "done deal."

- Tell you more about the company's culture, and whether or not you'd want to accept this job if you get an offer.

- Cause your interviewers to actively move the interview process to the next stage.

Asking "Power Questions"

In general, only one candidate in ten asks these "Power Questions"—and virtually every candidate who *does* ask them makes a powerfully positive impression. Here is each question, followed by a brief explanation of what you'll accomplish when you ask it:

"What are the first tasks you need the person in this position to address?"

This question subtly shifts your interviewers' viewpoint, by creating a mental picture of you already performing the job. In effect, you're changing the interview team's mindset from "Should we hire this person?" to "When this person is on board, what do I want him or her to be doing?"

"Is there anything that the person in this position will need to address immediately?"

This question highlights your concern for the company and your willingness to take on problems and solve them. It's even more powerful if you can follow it up with a specific example of a similar problem you've solved. For instance, you'll score major points if the interview team says, "Our client files are a mess and we need them fixed immediately" and you respond, "That'll be no problem—I once reorganized the entire filing system for an office of three lawyers in only two weeks."

"Are there any particular challenges involved in getting this project completed successfully?"

This question demonstrates that you don't just want to *do* the job—you want to *succeed* at it.

"What did you experience in your first few weeks here?"

This deceptively simple but powerful question accomplishes two key goals. It tells you what to expect if you get this position, and at the same time enables you to bond with your interviewer by encouraging him or her to share personal experiences.

"Do you find that employees are expected to work overtime occasionally, or are fifty- to sixty-hour work weeks the norm?"

This question is an excellent barometer of a company's culture—and it's one you need to ask these days, as too many companies are trying to improve their bottom line by overworking their employees. But be careful to phrase the question in a neutral way rather than making it personal (e.g., don't say, "Is your staff required to work fifty- to sixty-hour weeks?") You don't want to make your interviewer defensive.

"Can you explain how I will report to or interact with other managers, and other offices or locations?"

Asking this question will show the interview team that you understand the importance of interacting effectively with the entire organization, not just your direct reporting manager. In addition, the answer will provide you with information about the company's structure that will be critical to getting off on the right foot if you get the job.

"How would my performance be measured?"

This question puts you in the big leagues by demonstrating that you're planning to be a top performer. Few people ask this question, because few people think of it. In fact, your interviewers are likely to hesitate before responding, and they may not have a response to give you. But I guarantee you that the interview team will talk about this question at the end of the day, and give you credit for thinking enough about your future job performance to ask it.

"What are there opportunities for advancement for employees who meet or exceed their objectives?"

This is a solid question to ask, if you're interested in moving up the career ladder. It lets you know where you stand, and shows the interview team that you're thinking about a long-term future with the company.

"What are you looking for in the person you hire for this position?"

This is an excellent wrap-up question. If you've successfully used your interview to show how you're a perfect match for the job, this question will cause your interviewers to articulate all of the reasons why they should hire you.

How to Find Out Where You Stand

Interviews frequently end on a vague note, with the interview team merely saying, "Thanks, we'll get back to you." This is far from ideal from the candidates' standpoint, because it leaves them in limbo.

To avoid this scenario, wrap up your interview questions by asking, "Based on the conversation we've had to this point, do you feel that I'd be a match for the position?" You'll politely force your interviewers to play their hand, at least in a limited way, and you'll have a far better idea of whether they're interested in you or not.

Asking this question, whether the answer is positive or negative, will also improve your chances of getting the job. If you get a positive answer to your inquiry, you will have nudged your interviewers one step closer to a commitment. If the reply is negative or at best noncommittal, you'll have one more opportunity to identify problems and address them effectively. Be forthright and say, "If you have any particular areas of concern, I'd be glad to take a few more minutes and address them."

Assuming that the company expresses interest in you, also ask, "What is your timeline for filling this position?" and "What are the next steps in the process?" These questions will encourage your interviewers to keep the hiring process in motion.

And last, but not least, do what very few job seekers do: If you like the job, say so! Tell your interviewers, "I want you to know I'm very interested in the position. I look forward to the next step." Or, if this is the only interview you'll have, say, "If I'm selected, when can I begin work?" This positive and assertive approach takes courage, but it will brand you as a serious contender in the eyes of your interviewers.

After Your Interview . . .

When you get home, think about how your interview went, and make some notes in your files about how you can improve your performance. Also, take a few minutes to write a quick e-mail to your contact, thanking him or her for the opportunity to interview. If you realize that you forgot to mention a crucial point during your interview, you can make up for the oversight by including this point in your e-mail. Once you're done with these post-interview tasks, take a few hours off—you've earned a break!—but then get right back to your direct-calling campaign, if you haven't completed it yet. The interview you just finished is proof that your plan is working, so keep your momentum going. If you do, it won't be long until you reach the next stage: getting a job offer.

CHAPTER EIGHT

What If They Say Yes? What If They Say No?

Your first reaction, when you get a job offer, will probably be "Hallelujah!" Even in today's competitive job market, however, you shouldn't say yes immediately. This chapter will show you how to calculate your needs before you get an offer; how to counter an offer that isn't good enough; and how to determine the real value of the package your potential employer is offering. In addition, you'll learn how to respond if a company says "no," and how you can turn that rejection into a constructive experience.

L et's start with the "good news" scenario first, because at some point in your job search it WILL happen. It might take one, two, three, or more interviews, but eventually one of your target firms will give you a job offer. In fact, with luck and the help of your aggressive direct-calling campaign (see Chapter Five), you could find yourself weighing offers from two or three different firms.

A key piece of advice to remember when you have one or more offers is: *Don't stop looking for additional opportunities until you sign on the dotted line.* Interviews are grueling, but if you have multiple irons in the fire you'll feel far more comfortable during your job negotiations.

A second piece of advice is to recognize that today's business climate is different than that of the late 1990s, and that almost all the changes work in your employer's favor rather than yours. To know if the offer you're getting is great or substandard, you'll need to know what you can command today—and the answer, unless you're in health care or other high-demand fields, may be "not as much as you're worth."

The saying that "everything is negotiable" is still true in many facets of life, but it's not always true for job offers in today's world. Even the basics—a forty-hour week, health and life and disability insurance—are no longer guaranteed. That's why it's vital to do your research and network with other people in your career field to determine what you can realistically expect in the way of salary and benefits. There can be a tendency these days for candidates to dismiss the first offer they get, saying, "I can do better than that"—only to find out that in some cases, there is no "better" out there.

Conversely, a challenging job market doesn't mean that you need to settle for a bad job. There are many excellent employers, and increasing numbers of them are once again beginning to offer good (although usually not extravagant) wages and benefits. Don't expect a 1999 package if you're not in a high-demand field, but unless you're down to the wire financially and don't have any choice, don't accept an offer that you know you'll regret.

Last, but not least, don't entirely rule out negotiating. The next few sections will go through each part of a job offer, and explain what's negotiable and what's not—and just how far you can go.

What Are You Worth?

The best way to determine your value in today's job market is to talk with peers and colleagues who are in the same field as you. Get a picture, in addition, of the types of benefits, perks, and vacation time they're getting. Also, use the salary calculators at Web sites such as these to learn the typical rates for your skills in your area:

- Salary.com
- Careerbuilder.com
- Monster.com

Supplement this information by checking the job board listings for your type of job, and noting the salaries being offered. It's important to re-evaluate your worth in the marketplace every time you look for a new job, even if it has only been a year or two since your last job search. It's amazing how fast external factors—for instance, the rapid outsourcing of manufacturing jobs, or the jump in the need for health care workers as the Baby Boomer generation ages—can change the salary picture for an entire field.

Is That Offer as Good as It Looks—And Can It Get Better?

With good jobs currently in short supply in a number of fields, you might be tempted to say, "Yes!" the instant you get an offer. But resist the urge. Instead, analyze the offer carefully to see if it truly meets your needs, and look for potential weaknesses. (For instance: Does the "negative" of poor medical benefits outweigh the "positive" of a high salary?) Also, determine if any of the following parts of the offer could be open to negotiation.

The start date

This is usually the first point you'll agree on. Generally, the company will want you to start right away. You, on the other hand, will want to start when it's convenient for you.

Usually it's easy to smooth over this difference. The company isn't going to fall apart if you arrive two weeks from now, and they know it. In reality, their primary worry is that you'll get another offer in the interim, and ditch them. Assure them that you're on board, and they're likely to go along with your timetable.

Salary

This is a tough one, particularly in fields where employers are calling the shots. Nearly every company has a structure of grade levels, and a salary range for every position. This information is confidential, and highly guarded. However, it's an almost universal ploy to offer you a salary that's slightly below what they're actually willing to pay. Thus, there's good reason to counter the first offer with one that's slightly higher. If you've done your research on salary ranges for your industry and position then you should be prepared to counter effectively.

─────────── TALE from the TRENCHES ───────────

In Kansas, a recent college graduate with a nontechnical B.S. or B.A. degree can expect an entry-level job and a salary range of about $29,950 to $41,520, with the midpoint being $34,600. If you're in this position, a company will probably come in with an offer that's slightly below the midpoint—say, $32,000. Knowing that there's typically a $15,000 spread between the minimum and maximum offer for a grade level, you can counter with a figure that's $3,000 to $5,000 above the firm's offer. As you climb higher on the corporate ladder, the gap between minimum and maximum salary grows wider. For example, the range for a director-level position can run from a minimum of $72,080 to a midpoint of $90,100 to a maximum of $108,120—a spread of nearly $38,000. In such a situation, if your first offer is near the midpoint, see if you can raise it by eight to ten thousand dollars.

The offer you get will depend on a number of factors, some related to your skills and experience and some intrinsic to the company itself. They include:

- Your track record. If you're a new graduate, you'll generally be offered a lower salary than if you have five or six years of job experience.

- What the company is currently paying other new hires for similar positions.

- How pivotal the position is and how many other candidates are available.

- The type of company. Some firms set their salaries in stone, while small start-ups frequently lack the budget to be flexible on salaries. Small to midrange companies that are posting healthy profit numbers can often be talked into sweetening a salary offer.

- How many employees are already doing similar jobs. A firm can't afford to offend current staffers by offering new hires a markedly higher salary, so maintaining salary equity is a goal of many HR departments. You're likely to have better luck if no one else in the company is doing a job similar to yours, or if you're one of the first people hired in your category.

No matter how your company scores on these counts, it's smart to make a counteroffer—as long as it's not unrealistic. At worst, the company will say "sorry," and they might feel compelled to make up for that turndown by offering some other incentive.

The key, in asking for a higher salary, is to offer a compelling reason. This can be the experience you bring to the company, or the fact that the going rate for your skills is higher than what the firm is offering. Avoid using personal reasons, such as, "I can't meet my house payment on that salary." Instead, keep the discussion professional, and be sure to word your counteroffer in a positive way by saying, for instance, "I'd love to work here and I know I could contribute a great deal. Is this salary offer something we can negotiate?"

If you have competing offers, you can use one offer as leverage to improve another—but be careful when you play this game. Again, be positive. For instance, say, "I do have another offer, but I prefer the work you're doing and I'm really enthusiastic about being a part of your firm. However, they're offering me a significantly higher salary. Is there a possibility that you can meet or exceed their offer?"

The job title

There's little latitude here until you reach a senior level. However, since your benefits and salary are likely to be tied to your title and salary, it's worth your while to ask. As an example, you may be able to get the title of "Senior Financial Analyst" rather than merely "Financial Analyst." Again, however, you'll need to have compelling reasons for asking. This could include that that you held that title in your previous job or that the duties you're being asked to perform are commensurate with a better title than the company is offering.

Bonus or incentive pay

Here again, you'll have more chance of success if you're at a high level in your profession, or if you're in a performance-for-pay position such as sales. If so, ask if the company has higher ranges of incentive pay for higher performance, or for exceeding performance objectives.

Signing bonus

Once common, a signing bonus can be hard to get in today's market. Your odds are far better if you're currently employed and can show that leaving your existing job would cause you a specific financial hardship—for instance, if you need to relocate, or would forfeit your stock vesting.

Time off for previously scheduled vacations

Here's a perk you can often get if you ask. If you've already scheduled a trip to Yosemite or a visit to England, ask your new employer if you can take time off without having it deducted from your vacation time. Nine times out of ten, you'll get your way, because this is a relatively cheap way for your new firm to make you happy. Also, most companies already have provisions in place for such requests. And if you have "must-do" events scheduled, it's far better to inform your new bosses now than to spring this on them after you're hired. At this point, it looks assertive; later on, it will look unprofessional.

Time off without pay

Ask for this option if you've asked unsuccessfully for time off with pay for a previously scheduled event (see above). This also is a concession a new company will often make if you are coming from an employer or a position that offered you more vacation/personal time than what they are able to offer you as a new employee.

Reimbursement for work done at home

If you can demonstrate that you frequently work from home, companies will sometimes pay for the Internet connection, long distance calls, faxes, office supplies, and postage used out of your home office, as long as these expenses are work-related and documented. With businesses trying to break productivity records, few bosses will say "no" to someone who wants to do additional work! But make sure you have a specific idea in mind when you suggest this arrangement. If you make a vague request, you'll come off as someone who wants free stuff without a specific "deliverable" in mind.

Stock options

Ask if the company offers stock options, and find out if these are based on performance, grade level, or other criteria. If stock options aren't automatically offered, ask if you can receive them based on your performance. One caution, however: Be skeptical if a start-up company offers you stock options in lieu of crucial benefits. Remember that a stock option in a failed company is worth zero.

Relocation reimbursement

Here again, you're likely to get this perk only if you're at a high grade level—and the higher you are, the better the package should be. If you've already moved to a new city, but your household items are still stored elsewhere, see if you can be reimbursed for having them transported to your new location. (Just remember that such reimbursements are often seen as taxable income by Uncle Sam.) Also, ask if the firm will cover temporary living expenses while you're looking for a new home. These can include meals, lodging, car rental, and other necessities.

Severance pay

Asking about severance pay when you're offered a job seems a little like asking about a prenuptial agreement when your suitor says, "Will you marry me?" At this point, you're probably hoping to be with your new company for years to come, and you don't want to sound negative. Realistically, however, the market is volatile and odds are you'll be looking for another position in five years or less. For people in many fields, it currently takes an average of one month for every $10,000 of income to find a new job—and that can add up to a long time to get by on nothing more than unemployment insurance. So consider bringing up the subject—especially if you're in a field such as software programming, in which layoffs are common and new jobs can be hard to find—but ask for a severance pay guarantee only if you've reached a fairly high level in your profession, and feel that you're in a good position to negotiate. If you can, get a guarantee of at least two weeks of severance pay, or, if you're being offered an executive position, at least two months' worth if you are released in your first year of employ. You'll thank yourself later on.

High level perks

If you've reached the director level or above, you may expect more perks as part of your package. Among the extras you can negotiate if you're being offered an executive position:

- A car allowance or company-leased vehicle

- Low-interest or interest-free forgivable loan for twelve months

- A special class of stock options at extremely low strike prices

- An enhanced package of insurance benefits

Other perks can include additional time off or paid memberships to golf courses or country clubs—particularly if you can prove that you'd be doing business entertaining there.

Analyze the Benefits Package You're Offered

Before accepting a job offer, ask probing questions about the insurance plans the firm offers and how generous they are. The days of extravagant, fully paid plans are over in most fields, but you need to at least guarantee that you'll get the basics.

Unless you have private insurance, your package should include medical and long-term disability insurance. Ideally, your firm should also offer dental, vision, life, and short-term disability insurance, or at least give you the option of buying into these through a company plan. However, in real life, many companies (including big ones) forego anything other than medical insurance.

In most cases, a company will expect you to pay at least part of the cost for your medical and/or dental coverage. Find out how much, and don't settle for a vague answer. Also find out if the company plan offers a "preferred provider" option as well as an HMO. If you or a family member has health issues, the difference can literally be a life-or-death issue. A preferred provider plan offers coverage if you need to see specialists outside the plan, while an HMO limits you to providers within the plan and may be far more restrictive about the treatment options it will cover.

Also find out how quickly you become eligible for medical benefits. If you won't receive immediate coverage, see if you can negotiate to have the new firm cover the costs of your existing insurance until your new plan kicks in.

Evaluate other aspects of the benefits package carefully. Most medium-sized or large companies offer their employees 401(k) plans, although the percentage of firms that are willing to match your investment is shrinking. Find out if your potential employer has a 401(k), and, if so, how long you must wait before joining it and whether the company will match some or all of your contributions.

The best benefit plans are "cafeteria" plans, which let you pick from a selection of benefits. Under these plans, you get a certain number of points to "spend" on benefits. You can choose, for instance, or, to give up short-term disability insurance for stock options.

Before signing a job offer, ask for copies of the company's benefit plans and read them carefully. Also, make sure to obtain written documentation of whatever you're able to negotiate regarding your benefits. Decide which benefits are vital and which are of no interest to you. If you're planning on leaving a current job to take a new one, compare the benefits package that each firm offers.

When you do sign a job offer, make sure you keep a copy of the finalized agreement. File it, along with all of the paperwork on your benefit plans, somewhere where you can get your hands on it easily.

Should You Sign a Noncompete Agreement?

This is a contract between you and your employer, saying that you won't work for a direct competitor for a certain period (for instance, two years) after you leave your job. It's a fair request, because a company can't afford to have employees giving away its secrets to its rivals.

If you're asked to sign a noncompete agreement, it generally makes sense to do so—but first, read it carefully to make sure the terms are reasonable. While unfair noncompete agreements are very difficult for companies to enforce, they can cause you unnecessary grief.

If the position you're offered is with a consulting firm, you're in a slightly different position. In this case, find out how long you're prohibited from going to work directly for the companies to which the firm sends you. This could make a big difference down the road, if a company decides that they love you but not the consulting firm you're working through. If the terms seem onerous—for instance, if you're prohibited from working directly for a firm for three or four years after leaving your consulting job—ask for a shorter time period.

Weigh the Intangibles

Money is important, but so is the ability to be happy, to learn, to grow on the job, and to have time for your family or other outside interests. What you want out of a job, of course, will depend on your own needs and goals. Maybe you're raising four-year-old twins, and need to be home for dinner by 6:00 each night. Maybe you're seeking training in new skills, to increase your value on the job market. Maybe you hate freeway traffic. Or perhaps you're ambitious and aiming for a management position by the time you reach age thirty.

Think about what's important to you using the list that follows, and then evaluate how well a job offer meets these needs. If you're employed and debating whether to take a new position, also evaluate your current job and see how it stacks up against your new offer.

What Do You Want from Your Job?

Professional Goals:

- ❏ I want to learn new skills.

- ❏ I want to obtain more training.

- ❏ I want the opportunity to advance to a higher-level or management position.

- ❏ I want to have more authority.

- ❏ I want to have more autonomy/freedom/independence.

- ❏ I want the opportunity to be part of a team.

- ❏ I want to do challenging work.

- ❏ I want to work in a less stressful environment.

- ❏ I want to work in a more casual environment.

- ❏ I want job security.

- ❏ I want to work for a company with growth potential.

- ❏ I want to work in an industry with growth potential.

❐ I want the opportunity for increased salary/benefits.

❐ Other: _____

Lifestyle goals:

❐ I want a job that does not require extensive overtime.

❐ I want a job that does not require travel.

❐ I want a job that does not require me to work weekends/ nights.

❐ I want a shorter commute.

❐ I want the opportunity to telecommute.

❐ I want good benefits for myself/my family.

❐ I want more vacation time.

❐ I want to work for a company that is understanding about letting employees take time off for special family events or family crises.

❐ Other: _____

What If Your Current Company Asks You to Stay?

When you decide to leave one job for another, there's a chance your current employer will try to make you change your mind. If your boss comes to you and makes you an offer, what should you say?

It depends. More than 90 percent of the time, employees who accept counteroffers wind up leaving a company within a year, because the same problems that drove them to change jobs in the first place are still there. Also, counteroffers tend to poison the atmosphere. There's an assumption that if the company has to "bribe" you to stay then you're less loyal and less dependable than other workers.

However, if you're on the fence about your new offer, you still like your old company, and it's simply a matter of a single issue—you need a higher salary to make ends meet, or you deserve a promotion that's been slow in coming—then don't shut the door entirely. Consider the counteroffer, but do bear in mind that your relationship will be different than before if you accept it.

Exit Gracefully

If you're leaving your company to accept a new job, go out of your way to depart on a positive note. There's a good chance that you'll encounter some of your colleagues later on in your career, and they could be in a position to either help you or harm you.

Be tactful when you inform your boss that you're leaving, and, if possible, time your departure to cause your company the least inconvenience. Offer your boss a formal letter stating the date on which you will be resigning, and say that you've appreciated the opportunity to work with him or her. In fact, make a point of bringing up some positive aspect of your professional or personal relationship— for instance, "I really appreciate how you've always gone out of your way to help me learn new skills." Then, ask what you can do to aid in making your departure as painless as possible for the company. If you're asked to participate in an exit interview, be honest, but tactful, about why you're leaving.

What if Your Job Interview Results in a "No?"

So far, we've looked at the best-case scenario, in which your interview leads to a job offer. But there's a good chance, in today's competitive job market, that one or more of your interviews will result in a call or e-mail saying, "Thanks, but we picked someone else."

The first thing to realize is that this isn't always the end of the game. You'd be surprised how often the runner-up for a job winds up getting the position, and there are steps you can take to increase the odds of this happening to you.

TALE from the TRENCHES

Early on in my career, I interviewed for a position as Manager of Sales Recruiting for a large corporation. I made it to the final round, but I came in second to another candidate who accepted the position. It was tough to hear that someone else got the job I had wanted. However, I wanted to close out the interview process on a positive and professional note. So I followed up by contacting the vice president who had interviewed me, and I told him that I'd appreciated the opportunity to be considered for the position. I also asked him to let me know if anything changed, and to keep me in mind for future opportunities. A few days later, I received a call I didn't expect. A contact at the company informed me that the candidate they had selected decided to stay in his existing job. My caller asked, "Are you still available?" I was, and as a result, I wound up getting an excellent job.

Keep your cool and show your professionalism if your interviewing company calls to say they've decided upon another candidate. Remember, too, that employment isn't a static situation. Things change rapidly in today's business climate, and the company that didn't hire you today could very well call you next month. It's also possible that an interviewer who turned you down will be impressed enough to pass your name on to a peer in another firm who's hiring. You'll increase the odds of these "second chance" scenarios occurring if you accept your initial turndown with class and good grace.

Doing so, by the way, will separate you from the majority of job seekers. A high percentage of people who get turned down for a job take the rejection quite personally, and they react in a hostile way when they get the news. This is a major mistake that can cost you dearly down the road. Avoid it, and instead score points by acting with dignity.

Also, once you get over the initial blow of a rejection, get yourself back in the game mentally. Your first response to a turndown will probably be to feel discouraged and wonder, "What's wrong with me?" In all likelihood the answer is "Nothing at all." There's a talent glut in a number of career fields today, and employers can often find a half-dozen or more top candidates for each opening. If it turns out that two or three candidates are equally outstanding (a common scenario), the choice often comes down to a mental flip of the coin by the interview team.

This means that if you're one of three virtually flawless candidates who interview for a job, the odds are only one-in-three that you'll get the nod. If you're one of two ideal candidates, you still have only a fifty-fifty chance. The reality is that with today's stiff competition, a great candidate can be turned down for one, two, three, or even a dozen positions.

The moral: Don't take a rejection personally. Do review what happened in your interview, and spot any areas where you can polish your performance. But don't dwell obsessively on any minor slip-ups you made, because it's a good bet they had nothing to do with the outcome of the interview. Instead, think about what happened, come up with a better strategy for next time, and move on.

Above all, don't get discouraged. That may sound like easy advice to give, and hard advice to follow, if you gave it your all and were told, "Sorry—we hired someone else." But each day of your job hunt is bringing you closer to victory, and that includes the days when you encounter setbacks. The direct-calling technique is virtually guaranteed to keep creating interview opportunities for you, and one of those interviews *will* lead to a new job.

Of course, when you do get a new position, you'll have yet another challenge: keeping it. In today's turbulent times, protecting yourself from layoffs and downsizing and outsourcing is a job in and of itself. In fact, there's no way to guarantee that you'll keep your new position for years—but as you'll see in the next chapter, there are positive steps you can take to make your foothold a great deal more secure.

PART

FOUR

Take Control of Your Future:
How to Enhance Your Job Security—
And Your Long-Term Career Security

CHAPTER NINE

Keeping Your New Job Once You Get It

To maximize your chances of keeping your job in an ever-changing economy, your best bet is make yourself as indispensable as possible—and you need to start as soon as you're hired. We'll discuss here the best ways to enhance your job security by clearly defining what your company expects from you, establishing effective communications with your manager, getting your superiors to fully commit to your objectives (and getting those objectives in writing), and protecting yourself against the unfair practices that can be all too common in today's workplace.

The fact that you used the direct-calling strategy to win your new job says that you're self-motivated, goal-oriented, and able to succeed at a challenging assignment. Thus we won't spend the following pages offering obvious rules for succeeding on the job (e.g., "Get to work on time."). Instead, this chapter will teach you how to transform yourself from a high-level performer to a company superstar—and how to protect your job in the process.

It's more important than ever to start out on the right foot in a new job, and to build on that foundation by making yourself a key player early in the game. That's because the most important rule in today's job market is that *there are no guarantees.* No matter how hard you work, and no matter how great a job you do, your job could be at risk because of the possibility of a merger, downsizing, or restructuring.

To minimize that risk, and maximize the chances that you'll stay with your company and rise in its ranks, you need to do more than work hard. You need to work "smart," and you need to establish a rapport with your supervisors and coworkers from day one. Here's how.

Know What Is Expected of You

In Chapter Seven, you were advised to nail down, during the face-to-face interview, the performance expectations for your new job. If you did this, you're in a good position to get right to work. If not, make it your first assignment. At the earliest chance—preferably before you start work—sit down with your supervisor, and make sure you both understand:

- What your initial tasks are.

- What priority to assign each task.

- What outcomes your boss expects.

- What interim deadline/performance objectives you need to meet.

When you're done, you'll know exactly what you're expected to deliver, and you'll know just what your boss's priorities are. As a result, you'll probably be more valuable in your first week than most people are during their first two months.

Are You a Victim of Bait-and-Switch?

Your odds of succeeding in your new job depend not just on you but also on your boss. Will he or she stick by the agreements you made before you signed on? Or will you get the bait-and-switch treatment? Sometimes a switch in job parameters is unavoidable and fully justified. Other times, however, supervisors intentionally misrepresent the scope or responsibilities of a job during the interview stage. In today's job market, you won't have much recourse if your boss pulls the bait-and-switch tactic. However, don't be a victim. If the transgression is serious, there's a distinct possibility that your new position might not work out. Keep your contact list "warm and ready" by continuing to add new names to your Company Research Worksheet and following up with hiring managers you've already had interaction with. That way, when the need arises, you'll be able to pick up your direct-calling campaign right where you left off.

Meeting expectations is a continuing process, so each time you receive a new assignment, get your boss to spell out exactly what's wanted. As time goes on, you may need to ask fewer and fewer questions—but always ask enough to gain a clear picture of your task. Also, if you're put in charge of a large or critical project, get your manager to outline the objectives of the project in an e-mail, and to commit to them. This will give you a documented record, and protect you later if there's any question about whether you achieved your goals.

Some jobs have clearly marked milestones and endpoints, but in others success is more subjective. If your job involves a high degree of creativity, for instance, it's particularly essential to get a feel for your boss's likes and dislikes, and to get frequent feedback (especially during your initial projects). Many a web designer or graphic artist loses a job simply because a beautifully designed and organized work is labeled by a supervisor as too tame, or too bold, or "I don't know . . . it's just not what I expected." That won't happen, if you have a firm idea upfront of what's expected of you.

Scope Out Your New Environment

Once you clearly identify your initial tasks and goals, it's time to consider a less tangible aspect of your job: your new culture. Changing jobs is like traveling to a new country, where the language and laws are different and you can quickly find yourself in big trouble for making the wrong gesture or saying the wrong word. Are you moving from a casual to a formal environment? Leaving a firm with an iron-fisted CEO to work for a touchy-feely boss? Moving from an "everyone for himself" firm to a team environment? If so, you'll need to adjust your behavior accordingly, to avoid getting off on the wrong foot.

When it comes to corporate culture, even the smallest misstep can get you in hot water. For example, one woman who'd previously worked as a manager for an informal, fun-loving company failed to notice that her new office was far more formal. Her new boss eventually complained about her desk (too cluttered with personal effects), clothing (too casual and trendy), and conversational style (too friendly). All of these characteristics—which her former laid-back employers considered advantages—became *dis*advantages in the new setting, and nearly cost the new manager her job. She could have prevented this embarrassing and potentially catastrophic situation simply by observing her coworkers and emulating their businesslike style.

A company's culture is the end result of multiple factors including the personality of the CEO, the number of employees, the age of the firm, whether it's family-owned or not, and the product it makes or services it delivers. Because of this, each firm has its own style and idiosyncrasies, and identifying them can save you grief. You can accomplish this by keeping your eyes and ears open, and tactfully asking your coworkers about the unwritten rules and expectations.

Get Your Messages Across

It's up to you to help ensure that the channels of communication between you and your manager are clear and functional. One step in this process is to determine what type of communication makes your boss comfortable. Some people are "talkers," and prefer speaking with you face-to-face or by phone. Others are "readers," who are more comfortable getting e-mailed updates. Pay attention to which style of communication suits your boss best, and follow his or her lead. The sooner you adapt to your boss's expectations in this regard, the better off you'll be.

Also, make sure you communicate the right information at the right time. Here are five common sense rules—the five "don'ts"—that you need to follow in order to make sure you're getting and sending the right messages:

1. **Don't let your boss get blindsided.** If you know bad news is coming, brief your supervisor as quickly as possible. It's even better if you can offer a potential solution.

2. **Don't be a stranger.** If you're an introvert, overcome your shyness when you're around your boss. The only way you can score points for your contributions, and be defended if problems arise, is to let your supervisor know what you're doing and why.

3. **Don't delay in responding to phone calls or e-mails.** Your supervisor needs to know that you're responsive to his or her needs, as well as the needs of other company personnel or clients. Remember that you communicate *for* as well as *with* your boss, and that how you treat any contact from the CEO to a complaining customer will reflect on both you and your supervisor. If you can't respond fully to a query right away, at least send a quick note acknowledging that you've received the message and that you are working on it.

4. **Don't send mixed signals.** When talking or e-mailing, be succinct and to the point. State your opinions concisely, and stand by them. When you offer your viewpoint, be tactful— for instance, say "Here's another way to look at it" rather than, "No, that's not right"—and try to marshal sufficient facts to back your beliefs. But say what you think, rather than weaseling.

   Conflict avoidance has become an art form in today's workplace, and people frequently say one thing and do another. But you'll enhance your reputation and earn the trust of your boss if you're a straight shooter.

5. **Don't be too buddy-buddy.** You're at work for a reason, and it's not to pal around or commiserate with your manager. Be friendly and open, but keep your communication professional. Efforts to cozy up to your boss will make your peers resentful.

   It's a misconception that playing up to the boss creates job security. In reality, it creates contempt. Bosses tend to exploit the vulnerability of those who are overly eager or fawning, because they know that they can pile work on such employees without providing any reward or praise. And in the end, such employees are just as likely to be laid off as anyone else—if not more so.

Clear communication is vital in any business relationship, but be especially alert for communication short-circuits if you have a "problem" boss. A difficult manager can put you in a bad position by failing to communicate exactly what's expected of you, or by failing to keep you in the loop during a project. When this happens, you're likely to be blamed when things don't go as expected. If you take pains to initiate communication at each stage of a project—and to document this communication carefully, if you sense the potential for trouble ahead—you'll make your position more secure.

Be Visible

In the movie *Office Space*, some of the best scenes involve Milton, the pathetic employee who's so unnoticed that no one even bothers to notify him when he gets fired. While Milton's plight is comic, it's not so funny if you find yourself working diligently and yet receiving little notice. You can prevent this scenario by actively putting yourself on the radar screen of managers and other key people at your firm.

There are a number of ways to make yourself visible in a company. One is to be visible *physically*, simply be onsite, even if you work at a firm that allows telecommuting. This is particularly important if mergers or downsizings are in the works, because it's easier to prove that you're working hard if you're right in front of your boss's eyes. Also, put in extra hours when your company needs you. While overtime shouldn't be the status quo, you should cooperate fully during "crunch times" by working late hours or taking work home.

In addition to making yourself visible, make your *work product* visible. A friend of mine once worked at a hospital employing three dieticians. All three of them competently performed the quiet task that hospital dieticians typically do: planning nutritious, good-tasting meals for the patients and staff. But they also became minor celebrities at the hospital, because they went above and beyond their job descriptions. One planned monthly theme meals for hospital staffers—for instance, a "luau day" that was a huge hit with the doctors. The other two put their heads together with the hospital's PR staff and came up with the idea of holding community bakeoffs using healthful foods. The resulting events, and the free bakeoff recipes provided by the dieticians, resulted in positive TV and newspaper publicity. The three dieticians spent many hours of their own time planning these extracurricular activities, but their efforts paid off by enhancing both the hospital's image and their own. Rather than being three replaceable cogs in a large machine, they became memorable personalities, and assured their job security.

Similarly, you can look for ways to stretch your job to include new responsibilities that will put you or your department in the spotlight. Do what's required of you, but also ask yourself:

- Can I think of a better/more efficient way to do this job?

- Can I take on additional work —and, in particular, work that my supervisor doesn't like doing?

- Can I do something creative that goes beyond the obvious duties of my job description?

Another way to increase your profile is to participate in any charities your company sponsors—for instance, by helping with a 10-K run, or working on a holiday food drive. You'll earn the goodwill of your manager, especially if your department scores points as a result of your efforts, and you'll create an opportunity to form close ties with people in other departments. This can benefit you later, particularly if you need to make a "lateral move" at some point in order to protect your job.

Stay Ahead of the Curve

Now more than ever, you need to safeguard your career by learning new skills and technologies, because what you know now is likely to be passé in a few years. At Hewlett-Packard, for instance, the "half-life" of some engineering skills is only eighteen months! The era in which you could get by for decades on the skills you learned in college is gone forever; as human resources expert Karen Ferguson says, "You have to change your skill set until the day you retire." The next chapter discusses at greater length the concept of lifelong learning as a career-security builder. For now, think about protecting your current job by:

- Reading journals in your field

- Taking classes in your field, or in other areas that add to your value (marketing, foreign languages, computer skills)

- Earning certifications in new skills

- Mastering new technology

Make sure your supervisor is aware of your new skills, and always be on the lookout for projects where you can put them to use. Keep redefining your job, in ways that expand your influence and make you more essential to the company.

Keep Your Own Metrics

The recruiting field is big on "metrics"—statistics about how many people are placed in jobs, how long they stay, and how well they do. These numbers allow recruiters and hiring managers to spot both good trends and trouble signs. This same approach can help you track your own job success, and identify weak spots where you need to kick up your efforts. It also can empower you, even in a tough job market, to negotiate a raise or a promotion at review time. If your job lends itself to concrete statistics, keep track of those numbers. Otherwise, every three to six months, make a list of:

- The projects you've successfully completed

- Milestones you've met—or failed to meet—and goals you've exceeded

- New duties you've taken on, or new skills/technologies you've mastered

- Ways in which you've streamlined company procedures, saved your firm money, or increased productivity

Use your answers to analyze how strong your job performance is. Also, compare your performance honestly to the achievements of coworkers doing similar assignments for your firm. Are you outshining them, or falling behind? The answer could determine whether you're the first one promoted, or the first to go in a layoff.

Say "No" to Office Politics

The world is full of job experts who tell you how to "swim with the sharks," and how to "squash the corporate cockroaches" that get in the way of your career advancement. But almost all the experts in the hiring-and-firing business will tell you that the best advice for getting ahead in your career is the simplest: Follow the Golden Rule.

You can play office politics, by gossiping and backstabbing, but these tactics only work in sick organizations with weak leaders. Instead, follow the suggestion of successful marketing firm CEO Jeffrey Fox, who recommends in *How to Become CEO*, "Don't waste your time. Spend your time creating and accomplishing. Let your actions be your politics. . . . Be the last to know. Don't get sucked in. Don't let people tell you something if they say it's 'confidential.' Don't gossip. Say, 'I don't know.'"

It's powerful advice, and it works. Some people do climb the corporate ladder on the backs of people they've crushed, but in general it's a self-defeating tactic. It's even more dangerous in today's business world, where you're likely to change jobs two or three times in the next decade—and you're likely to keep encountering old friends, and old enemies, who are in positions to make or break your chances.

Instead of spending time scheming against rivals or playing up to allies, do your job in a way that will allow you to look yourself in the mirror each morning. Compete not with your coworkers, but with yourself. And if you worry about "nice guys finishing last," consider that a large body of sociological research actually shows that followers of the Golden Rule are typically more successful in life than their selfish counterparts.

Of course, every once in a while, you'll encounter a coworker or boss who plays dirty—for instance, by taking credit for your work, or by trying to blame mistakes on you. When you run into such a person, resist the urge to fight back—but play smart, by being extra careful to document your own work and accomplishments, as well as to document any conversations or e-mails that could be critical in the future.

Be Realistic

Being a "good guy" doesn't mean that you should be naïve about your employers or about your future with them. In the harsh new reality of the workplace, neither nice guys *nor* bad guys can count on having any real job security. That's why it's smart to think, instead, of "career security."

What does that mean? Simply this: The days of holding one job for decades (or even for more than a few years) are over. They aren't coming back, either, at least in the foreseeable future. Instead, plan for long-term security by ensuring that you are ready—at any time of your life, and at any stage in your career—to use your acquired skills and experiences to find a new opportunity. In the next chapter, you'll learn how to stop leaving your fate in the hands of fickle employers, and take charge of your own career destiny.

CHAPTER TEN

The New Reality: Keep Looking, Even When You Have a Job

Job security is a thing of the past, and in today's world you'll be lucky to keep the same job for even a few years. The only way to stay ahead during a time of constant and highly unpredictable job market changes is to keep a keen eye on economic trends, corporate hiring and layoffs, and other data that can help you make the leap to a better job if your old one vanishes. Learn how to become your own recruiter by continually expanding your list of contacts, building relationships, and constantly maintaining and updating your corporate database.

Your grandparents—and your parents, if you're a Baby Boomer—could get hired right out of college and expect to retire decades later (often from the very same firm) with a gold watch, lifelong health insurance, and a hefty pension.

These days, however, you're lucky if you stay at a job for more than five years, and pensions and lifelong benefits are nearly extinct. It doesn't always matter how good you are, how loyal you are, or how much overtime you put in—because external forces, from globalization to technological changes, are claiming the jobs of vast numbers of America's best employees. As a result, the only constant today is job *instability*. The U.S. Department of Labor reports that the average worker will work for ten employers over a lifetime, keeping each job an average of three and a half years. You're also likely to change career fields three or more times before you retire.

─────────── TALE from the TRENCHES ───────────

One day, as I drove to a new firm where I'd just started a contract position, I heard on the radio that a competitor was launching a takeover bid for that company. Immediately afterward, the firm put large numbers of contracts and projects on hold, in preparation for the takeover. I didn't wait around for the bloodbath that eventually occurred. Instead, I immediately started getting in touch with my contacts, and lined up a new contract. My quick response saved me thousands of dollars in revenue, not to mention sparing me the stress of waiting for the axe to fall. If you find yourself in a similar situation, don't drag your feet. As quickly as you can, update your contact list, restart your direct-calling campaign, and see if you can score a new position before your current one becomes history.

Offshoring, automation, and an ever-fluctuating economy aren't the only reasons your job isn't secure. The entire relationship between employers and employees is changing radically, and it's leaving workers far more exposed than before. In earlier years, the unwritten social contract between employers and workers was that if you worked really hard for a company, and excelled at what you did, your company reciprocated by keeping you on through thick and thin, paying for your medical care, and making sure you retired with enough money to keep you comfortable. Now, however, the contract of all too many firms simply reads: *You're here as long as we need you, and then you're history.*

Of course, there still are great companies that care about their employees, nurture and train them, and believe that respect is a two-way street. Smart firms think long-term, and they recognize that key employees are vital assets. These companies support their workers through thick and thin, and do their best to treat them fairly and give them opportunities to advance.

For every firm that thinks this way, however, there's one that's willing to sacrifice its loyalty to workers for short-term profits. With the job market currently picking up, many of these companies will pay dearly for that strategy, when their most experienced and highest-level employees run for the doors. But because employers in many fields still hold the power right now, and will for at least a while to come, a significant number of firms will continue to discard employees like paper towels. No matter how wonderful your company seems or how high your corporate profit margin is, it's a mistake to think that you're immune from this trend.

Your first line of defense against being laid off, of course, is to make yourself as indispensable as possible (see Chapter Nine). But your second is to realize that there's actually no such thing as "indispensable," and respond by:

- Watching for signs of trouble at your current company

- Keeping your eye on the job market

- Constantly upgrading your own "employability"

In short, strange as it sounds, the way to survive in today's job world is to start looking for your next job even if you're happy in the one you just worked so hard to procure.

Keep an Eye on Your Company's Vital Signs

The first key to long-term career security is to monitor your company's health. If things take a major turn for the worse at your firm, you'll want to be ready to make a quick move, especially if the opportunities in your field are limited. Wait too long, and the coworker who leaves before you could grab the good job you want.

How can you tell when your job, or your entire firm, is in trouble? Sometimes you can't. Frequently, the first news of a crisis comes suddenly, because today's companies typically are tight-lipped until the last minute about the changes that will affect their employees.

While it's easy to be caught by surprise in today's unstable job world, more often than not you can spot subtle (or not-so-subtle) clues that layoffs or other crises are in the offing. That's why you need to keep your eyes open. The following fifteen situations are among the signs you should look out for.

Sign #1: Did the person who hired you leave?

If this happens, things are bound to change, and sometimes they change dramatically for the worse. I've placed many candidates in "perfect" jobs, only to receive calls (sometimes just a few weeks later) from those candidates, saying, "Help! I have a new boss who's ruining my life." If you find out that your current manager is leaving, be willing to give your new boss a fair trial—but also prepare for the possibility of a negative change.

Sign #2: Are other key players leaving?

If your company is starting to hemorrhage top management people and other high-value staff, there's probably a good reason for the exodus. See if you can find out why everyone's leaving, and where they are going. This is especially crucial if the people who are departing have a high opinion of you, and might be able to pull you into a new company with them.

Sign #3: Is a change of ownership in the offing?

It's a common scenario: One minute you're comfortably adjusting to your new role, and the next minute you hear that your employer is being purchased or merged with another company. This is disconcerting to say the least, especially if you've been through this process before. If you haven't, be forewarned: Do *not* believe your firm's assurances that nothing will change. In reality your projects, and possibly your job, are at risk—no matter how high up the management chain you are and how many years of seniority you have. At the first hint of a major ownership change, it's time to start putting out feelers.

Sign #4: Is there a change in reporting structure?

Sometimes a shake-up in the organizational chart can lead to disastrous consequences. In one such firm, the vice president of Human Resources brought in a new person to take over some of her responsibilities. Qualified internal candidates were overlooked in favor of the new hire, who had no experience whatsoever in HR, and within a one-month period the department experienced a 100 percent turnover. If you find yourself in a similar position, start looking for your next opportunity before things get grim.

Sign #5: Is the company's stock moving downward?

When stock prices drop, stockholders expect action—and often, that action comes in the form of layoffs, which allow CEOs to protect their own jobs while saying that they're cutting costs. If your firm is publicly owned, check its stock prices occasionally, and be aware of what experts are saying about its future potential. Minor bumps in stock prices are normal, but a long-term slide is a major red flag.

Sign #6: How is your industry as a whole doing?

If you see a pattern of business closures, layoffs, or outsourcing to other countries, assume that your job could be the next to go. If the situation is serious enough, start thinking about re-training to prepare yourself for other career options.

Sign #7: How is your division doing?

If your revenues are falling while other divisions are turning a profit, watch out for a restructuring that could send your entire team packing. Today's companies are more ruthless than ever about eliminating activities that don't bring in money.

Sign #8: How are your major clients faring?

If you're still turning out a great product, but the clients who use it are downsizing, outsourcing, declaring bankruptcy, or closing their doors, your company's future is insecure. Again, this is a situation in which you may need to consider changing careers in the near future.

Sign #9: Are the managers often locked away in secret meetings?

Bosses typically don't want their workers to get an early warning of major changes, particularly if those changes are negative. It's to their advantage to keep you happy, productive, and clueless until the day that they don't need you. Therefore, if layoffs or other problems are in the offing, you're likely to see company leaders holding frequent closed-door meetings, meeting off-site at unusual times, or returning very close-lipped from meetings.

Sign #10: Is there a "black hole" when it comes to new contracts or projects?

If you aren't in a position to know this, talk offline with the sales staff or other people who have knowledge of the company's financial picture.

Sign #11: Do you see evidence of cash flow problems?

For instance, is the accounting department paying bills late, when they always used to pay on time? Did a major contract with a huge firm get cancelled? Are you being asked to take a "temporary" pay cut, or to accept reduced benefits? (One exception: Don't be too alarmed if you're asked to pay more for your health benefits. With health insurance costs skyrocketing, even successful companies are asking their employees to share more of this burden.) Are employees, and especially those in high-paying jobs, being asked to take early retirement?

Sign #12: Are you being excluded from meetings you used to attend?

This often is a sign that management considers you irrelevant and could be planning to eliminate your job. Increase your efforts to make yourself valuable to your firm, but also start thinking about making a move.

Sign #13: Are your requests for help being denied?

When you ask for training, additional staff, or new equipment, are your requests rejected? If so, is this happening to everyone, or just to you? See if you can detect a pattern, and if it indicates that management is singling out you or your department.

Sign #14: Are you sensing strange vibes?

Other people—your boss, the HR staff—are likely to know you're being laid off long before you get the news. If you sense that these people are avoiding you or feel uncomfortable around you, it could be a hint that you're on your way out.

Sign #15: Are you being asked to prepare for outsourcing?

If so, look for a new job now. It doesn't matter if your company makes vague promises about keeping its hometown employees on board. Be polite and helpful when it comes to training your replacements—this will help when it comes to getting good references—but don't stick around any longer than you need to. Making the decision to leave a company where your prospects look dim is stressful, but it's almost always preferable to hanging on until the bitter end. By looking for a job while you still have one, you'll be in a better financial position to wait for the right offer—and you'll exchange "pink-slip anxiety" for a sense of control over your future.

Know When It's Time to Move Forward

During the course of your career, there will be times when you, and not your employers, make the decision that it's time for a change. With the job market perking up, now might be one of those times. If you're not satisfied with your current position, ask yourself if it's time to move on. In deciding, consider these questions.

Am I getting stale in this job?

If your current company offers no chances for advancement, and no training to upgrade your skills, it's time to consider a move. Staying at a dead-end job for another year or two could make it harder for you to get a good one in the future, because your skills will be out-of-date.

Is my current job an unpleasant place to be?

The recent recession kept many people trapped in jobs they hated, and allowed many employers to mistreat workers without fear of losing them. But times are changing and, with hiring on the rebound in many fields, the chances of escaping from such settings are growing better each day. If you work for a firm that expects you to put in endless overtime without compensation, to work in a bad physical environment, or to make do with few or no benefits and a salary that doesn't meet industry standards, it's time to start looking for greener pastures.

How to Post a Confidential Resume

A confidential resume might be the only safe way to advertise on the Internet. If so, be very careful. Delete your name and replace it with a job title—for instance, "Account Manager." Next, delete the name and location of your current employer, as well as any other identifying information, and simply give the firm a generic title (e.g., "large telecommunications firm"). Also delete any other information that could give away your identity—including any information embedded in the file. If shrouding your information to this degree sounds paranoid, consider that companies sometimes ask in-house or third party recruiters to scour the Internet for resumes of employees who are seeking new jobs. Often, an employer will get downright mean if it discovers that an employee is shopping around. So play it safe, and make sure your confidential resume truly *is* confidential.

If you are looking for another job while still in one, keep quiet about it. Don't even tell your close friends at work, because word will get back to your boss. The time to tell your colleagues or supervisors that you have a new job is when it's a done deal, and you don't need to worry about any repercussions.

Keep Your Eye on the Job Market

When the time does come to leave your current job—either because you've been let go or because you want a change—you'll be ahead of the game if you know who's hiring, who's turning a good profit, who's planning on outsourcing 500 jobs to India next month, who's in trouble with the SEC, or whose new product is expected to revolutionize your entire industry.

To keep up with such developments, continue the research you did in Chapter Four when you investigated target companies. Keep reading your local business journal and online business news, as well as the business section of your local paper, and follow the trends in your area and your industry. Also keep an eye on salary trends, so you won't overprice or underprice yourself when the time comes to interview again.

To get the most value from your ongoing research, *keep updating the Company Research Worksheet you developed in Chapter Four, even when you have a job.* As you uncover new facts about companies in your area, and spot information about potential contacts, enter these facts into your database. Then, when the time comes to find a new job (and in today's world, it's "when" and not "if"), you'll be ready to jump right into your search. In effect, this database, combined with your direct-calling skills, turns you into your own recruiter and frees you permanently from being dependent on other people to get a job.

Master the Art of "Circling Back"

In an insecure job world it's vital to develop and nurture your professional contacts as if your career depends on it, because it does. While networking isn't always an effective strategy during the intense phase of a job hunt, it's immensely powerful over the long term.

Too many people turn to their networks only when they're in trouble, and tend to forget them when life is stable. One candidate expressed it the following way, "I should be able to pick up the phone and get a job with any number of people I've worked with over the past years. But I just didn't bother to stay in touch, so now I don't feel comfortable parachuting back in and asking for help." This candidate's story is not unusual. How many times have you resolved to stay in contact with former coworkers, only to lose track of them?

From now on, follow through on your resolve by doing what I call "circling back." Remember to e-mail or phone your business contacts every few months, and arrange lunches or other get-togethers on occasion. Don't fall into the pattern of calling only when you need a favor; instead, let your contacts know that you're interested in how they're doing, and that you value them as friends or colleagues. Equally important, be there for your contacts when they need you. Seek out opportunities to help out the people in your network, even if it takes some effort on your part.

Another key networking tip is to be sure to get the home phone numbers or e-mail addresses of any colleagues at your current firm with whom you'd like to stay in contact over the long term. This way, if you and your colleagues are laid off at the same time, you'll be able to contact each other. Make sure you keep this information at home, and not just on your computer at work where it might be inaccessible if you're laid off.

Upgrade Your "Employability"

Combine an increasingly global work force with ever-improving technology, and you have the recipe for a fluid and unpredictable future. Will your job be heading to China in a year? Will your inventory job be turned over to a new software program? To be successful in a world with so many unknowns, you need to work hard to stay at the top of your game.

One of the smartest moves you can make is to get all the training you can. If possible, expand your responsibilities at your current firm to include new skills, and particularly those that are "hot" at the moment. If your company provides training, take advantage of this. New employers often expect an alphabet soup of skills, and the more you can add (within reason), the better off you'll be.

Also, if you don't have a degree in your field, look into getting one. If you have a B.A. or B.S., consider getting an advanced degree if it would improve your chances in the job market. Of course, plenty of Ph.D.s are out of work these days, so do your research and find out if a higher degree will truly improve your marketability in your career field. Some degrees can double your future pay, while others are a waste of time.

If your field offers certification programs, looking into getting certified in one or more skills—but don't automatically assume that this will get you a better job or more money. Employers generally rank experience as more important than a certification, but that piece of paper can sometimes give you an edge if there's close competition for a position.

Even if you're a nontechie, upgrading your computer skills will make you more marketable, because almost every job now involves using a computer in one way or another. Training in basic computer skills is often inexpensive or even free, through your local library or community college, and you can also find tutorials online.

If you have the time and the talent, consider learning a second language. Being bilingual is a big plus in today's labor market, especially if you can develop enough expertise to pass a certification exam. Pick the most common non-English language spoken in your community, or—alternately—a common "business" language, such as Japanese, that can be very valuable if you're hoping to score a job with a multinational corporation.

Don't feel constrained, however, to learn skills that directly relate to your current field. One advantage of lifelong learning is that you can explore new career fields and increase your financial security by becoming multitalented. Those who are trained in more than one field or have skills they can cross-sell find that there is almost no "down" job market for them. In an unpredictable age, in which you're likely to change career fields multiple times, being a Renaissance man or woman is a huge advantage.

What's Your Style— "Traditional" or "Emergent?"

"Emergent workers" are those who take control of their careers and expect to be rewarded for performance—not for long-term loyalty. They see job changing as a fact of life rather than an earth-shaking life crisis. In contrast, "traditional" workers expect their employers to pave their career paths for them. In return, these workers offer their bosses long-term commitment and loyalty. As the social contract dissolves between employer and employee such workers are in for a shock, if they haven't received one already. According to business trend researcher Chuck Martin, "We are in a world of every company and every individual for themselves." Savvy workers recognize this, and they're evolving rapidly from a traditional to an emergent philosophy. Based on a recent survey, the recruiting agency Spherion says that 31 percent of the workforce is now emergent, while only 21 percent is traditional. However, by 2007, emergent workers are expected to make up more than half of the U.S. workforce.

Plan Your Finances So You're Ready for the Future

Have you ever accepted a not-very-good job simply because you needed a paycheck right away? Nearly everyone takes a "desperation job" at some point, but it's an act you want to avoid whenever possible. If you can save up enough money to cover several months of job-hunting, you'll be able to keep your options open rather than grabbing desperately at the first offer you get. Also, when you do get a new job, try to get a guarantee of at least a few weeks of severance pay, to provide a cushion the next time around.

In addition to being your own recruiter, you'll need to be your own benefits representative because you'll probably encounter frequent changes in your medical, life, and disability insurance coverage. Become knowledgeable about COBRA, a government-mandated program that ensures (under certain conditions) that your health coverage with an employer is "portable"—that is, that you can continue your coverage on a self-pay basis if you're laid off. Check to see if the life insurance coverage you have through your firm is portable as well. And look into guilds and associations that can provide you with certain types of insurance coverage if you lose your job, or take a job that doesn't cover all of your insurance needs.

Assume Control of Your Destiny!

All of the responsibilities outlined in this chapter—updating your corporate database, researching industry trends, taking the pulse of your company on a regular basis, accepting responsibility for understanding your benefits, maintaining your network, keeping your job skills up-to-date—add up to a great deal of work.

The payoff for this effort, however, is well worth the cost. When you find the right job by using the Fifteen-Day Direct-Calling Campaign, and then follow that success with a long-term career-security plan, you'll place yourself squarely in charge of your own future. While your friends and colleagues worry about unemployment or struggle in dead-end jobs, you'll have the tools you need to get a new and better position at any moment—no matter how good or bad the job market is.

When you've mastered the techniques outlined in this book, you'll never again feel that you're helpless, with no control over the whims of a company that could downsize or outsource your job at any moment. Instead, you'll stay ahead of the game because you'll be ready, at any time, to set your direct-calling campaign in motion again. As a result, you'll eliminate the control that your employer has over your life, and instead place that control directly into the right hands: your own.

INDEX

A

administrative assistants, 83–85
alumni Web sites, 65
Annual Report Gallery, 63
Applicant Tracking Systems, 8

B

Baby-Boomer retirement, 4, 6
behavioral interviewing, 103–105
benefits packages, 142–144
Bizjournals, 63
bonuses, 139
business publications, 41
Business Wire, 65

C

calls: recording results from, 85–89;
    scenarios for, 80–85; scheduling,
    79–80; script for, 76–79; timing of,
    75–76. *See also* direct calling
call screeners, 83–85
candidates, screening of, 95–96
career changes, 24–25
career-marketing firms, 42–44
cell phones, 119
cafeteria plans, 143
civic clubs, 65
COBRA, 179
cold calling, 75

communication, with boss, 157–159
companies: focusing on needs of
    prospective, 100–103; identifying
    target, 49–66; monitoring health of,
    168–173; researching, 50–57
Company Research Worksheet, 52–57,
    70–71
competitors, 54
confidence, 74–75
contacts: identifying, 59. *See also* hiring
    managers; targets
corporate culture, 124–126, 156–157
CorporateInformation.com, 63
corporate Web sites, 38–39, 62
counteroffers, 146–147
culture, corporate, 124–126, 156–157

D

departure, from old job, 147
direct calling: difficulty of, 69–70;
    eliminates middle man, 21;
    impression left by, 21–22, 25–26;
    as key to getting hired, 17–20; vs.
    networking, 19; preparation for,
    49–66; reasons for effectiveness of,
    20–27; referrals generated by, 22–23;
    steps for successful, 70–90; success
    ratio for, 68–69; timing for, 75–76.
    See also calls

E

e-mail etiquette, 112–114
e-mail addresses, 33, 112
emergent workers, 178

F

finances, 179
401(k) plans, 143
Fullerman, Franklin, 56

G

Gateway for Associations Online, 64
Give.org, 64
globalization, 5, 165–166
goals: lifestyle, 146; meeting your, 71–74; professional, 145–146
Google, 59–61
Guidestar, 64

H

Heintz, Rich, 22
help-wanted ads, 41–42
Hiring Contact Status Report, 57–58, 71, 85–89
hiring managers: decisions by, 20–21; direct calling of, 17–19; making impression on, by direct calling, 21–22; timing for contacting, 75–76
hiring process: changes in, 6–11; problems with, 12. *See also* job-search techniques
Hoover's Online, 62
hostile questions, 122–124
human resource departments: bypassing, 18–19; resumes read by, 7–8

I

incentive pay, 139
industry conferences, 65
Industry Research Desk, 63–64
IndustryWeek, 63
insurance benefits, 142–143, 179
Internet research, 59–66
interviews: assessing corporate culture during, 124–126; attaining, 90–91; behavioral, 103–105; common questions on, 103–108; face-to-face, 115–132; handling hostile/tricky questions on, 122–124; phone, 95–110; post-interview tasks, 131–132; preparing for, 97–98, 116–121; questions to ask during, 108–109, 127–131; stress, 122–123; thank-you notes after, 111–112; tips for acing, 121–122; unsuccessful, 148–150; visual displays for, 119–121

J

job boards, 10, 34–38
job expectations, 154–156
job interviews. *See* interviews; phone interviews
job market: current state of, 4–6; factors affecting, 4–5; monitoring, 174–175
job offers, 133–146; benefits packages in, 142–144; counteroffers, 146–147; evaluating your worth and, 135; intangibles in, 144–146; negotiating, 135–142; noncompete agreements and, 144; recognizing good, 134–136
job openings, unadvertised, 20
jobs: deciding to change, 173–174; succeeding in new, 154–164

job search consulting firms, 42–44
job search goals: meeting your, 71–74
job-search techniques: to avoid, 42–45;
    changes in hiring process and, 6–11;
    ineffectiveness of traditional, 15–16;
    traditional, 29–30. *See also* direct
    calling
job security, 153–154, 164–168
job titles, 138–139

M

medical benefits, 142–143, 179
metrics, 162
motivation, maintaining your, 89–90

N

networking, 11, 175–176; vs. direct
    calling, 19; tips for, 39–41
newspaper ads, 41–42
newspapers, 64
noncompete agreements, 144
nonverbal communication, 121

O

office politics, 162–164
online applications, 8
online research, 59–66, 59–66
outsourcing, 5, 165–166

P

performance expectations, 154–156
perks, 142
phone interviews, 95–110; common
    questions on, 103–108; manners for,
    99; preparing for, 99–100; questions

to ask during, 108–109; as screening
    tool, 95–98; thank-you notes after,
    111–112; tips for, 100–103. *See also*
    interviews
productivity, increased, with fewer
    workers, 4–5

Q

questions: to ask interviewers, 108–109,
    127–131; behavioral, 103–105;
    common interview, 103–108; deal-
    breaker, 108–109; hostile/tricky,
    122–124; inappropriate, 123; power,
    128–130; salary, 109–110

R

recruiters, 8–9, 42
references, 10, lining up, 98; offering,
    110
referrals, 22–23
rejection, 69, 89, 148–150
relocation reimbursement, 141
research: Company Research Worksheet,
    52–57; as first step in job hunting,
    50–51; for interviews, 116–118;
    ongoing, 174–175; tips for online,
    59–66
resumes: gaps in, 107; to job boards,
    34–38; keywords on, 33–34; posting
    confidential, 174; reviewing, prior
    to interview, 118; sent to human
    resource departments, 7–8; tips for
    writing, 31–34
resume spamming, 16, 44–45
rewards, 90

S

salary, 134; negotiating, 136–138;
    questions, 109–110
scripts, rehearsing, 76–79
search engines, 59–61
severance pay, 141–142
signing bonuses, 139
skilled workers, demand for, 3–6
skills, keeping current, 161, 176–178
start dates, 136
Stein, Marky, 17
stock options, 140
strengths: identifying your, 107;
    showcasing your, 23–24
stress interviews, 122–123

T

targets, identifying, 49–66
telephone interviews. *See* phone
    interviews
thank-you notes, 111–112
time off, 139–140

trade journals, 41
training, for new skills, 176–178
trick questions, 122–124

V

vacation time, 139–140
Vault, 62
visibility, 159–161
voice mail, 80–83

W

weaknesses, identifying your, 108
Web sites: for company information,
    62–66; corporate, 38–39, 62
worker dissatisfaction, 13
work from home arrangements, 140
worth, evaluating your, 135

Y

Yahoo Corporate Reports, 63